HISPANICS' EDUCATION AND BACKGROUND

Predictors of College Achievement

Richard P. Durán

College Entrance Examination Board, New York 1983

To Winton H. Manning, in recognition of his continuing leadership on behalf of Hispanic higher education.

Contents

Tables

Figures

Foreword

It has been more than fifty years since Dr. George Sanchez published his warning that native Spanish-speaking children should be evaluated differently than should native English speakers, if educators are genuinely interested in measuring cognitive development. Dr. Richard Durán has written a careful, thorough review of nearly every published research study on Hispanic college achievement, and this review will properly serve as the major work on Chicano and Puerto Rican achievement until additional work is undertaken by psychologists.

This is not damning the book with faint praise. It is an excellent source book and synthesis, and Durán's own scholarship is first-rate. Someone had to synthesize the fugitive work done over the years, often done badly, and propose a research agenda for this generation of scholars, particularly Latino psychologists. Durán has done this unenviable task and has distilled the validity studies, demographic data, and psychometric research into a readable understandable whole. The chapter on demography is particularly good often more helpful than the original works. Moreover he took care in explaining flaws in earlier studies and in extracting important findings rendering his judgments fair and balanced.

Durán has decided not to take his own careful review to its logical end: the role of testing and the testing industry in the context of children not measured. In his own understated words, "The question of how to conceptualize achievement in college is nontrivial." Indeed! It is particularly "nontrivial" when "at present there exists contradictory and diverse views on the value of tests as predictors of Hispanics' college achievement." In fact, Durán's review found that almost every study conducted showed noticeably lower correlations between standardized admissions tests and first-year college grades for Hispanos, relative to Anglos. Given the extraordinary high school attrition rate for Hispanic children and the likelihood that the very best survivors are taking tests, he is generous towards those who would employ these tests uncritically in admissions decisions.

The condition of Hispanic education has demonstrably worsened over time, even as more Hispanic children enter and graduate from elementary and secondary schools. Even with more visibility of Hispanic children and issues, school systems, colleges, and professional organizations have not integrated their professional ranks. Overwhelmingly

Hispanic schools remain majority male in their leadership, while virtually no Hispanics hold significant positions in postsecondary institutions. This inequity cannot continue, and while Durán's work does not pose solutions to this problem, his suggestions on improving Hispanic research will surely improve societal awareness of the extent of the problem. Increased research is essential, and Durán correctly points to psychometrics and testing evaluation as urgently-needed priorities.

This agenda brings me full circle to Dr. Sanchez. To his sorrow, Sanchez's criticisms were never taken as seriously as they should have been, and the grounds of bilingual education have shifted to litigation and politics, not linguistics and research. Therefore, this analysis may not reach the necessary audience. It would be a shame if this thoughtful, provocative work did not stimulate debate on the efficacy of minority testing. Advocates on both sides had better familiarize themselves with this book. Sanchez's careful work has become the intellectual framework for Durán's book, and it is for the rest of us to press institutions and testmakers for accountability on Hispanic access issues.

Michael A. Olivas
Associate Professor of Education and Law
Director, Institute for Higher Education and Law
University of Houston
January 1983

Preface

The investigation of what factors underlie ethnic minorities' opportunities to attain and succeed in higher education is an inductive enterprise that has no absolute beginning or end. In terms of social science analyses of what factors influence educational attainment, the wise are quick to understand that there are no simple answers. Particular background factors, such as ethnicity or minority group status, do not fully explain the conditions of life that cause some people to achieve more educationally than others. Attempting to understand why U.S. Hispanics succeed or fail to attain higher education is an example of such a circumstance. As will be amply demonstrated in the first chapter and throughout this report, there is little doubt that Hispanics do not benefit from the U.S. educational system as much as nonminorities do. Further, Hispanic identity in the U.S. is often linked with factors that directly or indirectly restrict access to and achievement in higher education. A simplistic and culturally chauvinistic interpretation of the situation would conclude that Hispanics' educational attainment is a function of their ability or inability to adopt the sociocultural values and language of mainstream America. An equally naive view, at another extreme, would be that failure of Hispanics to succeed and continue in school is due *exclusively* to prejudicial bias against Hispanics in the educational system and to deliberate exclusion of Hispanics from educational institutions. The present report does not adopt or support either of these extremes, or other equally polarized views. The main goal of this review is to document existing evidence on issues in as impartial a fashion as seems feasible, given the comments that follow.

The report reviews issues and previous empirical studies surrounding prediction of U.S. Hispanics' college achievement as represented by college grades. The association of basic demographic characteristics with educational attainment and preparation for college is considered. Special attention is given to achievement data on Hispanic high school students and to college admissions test scores of students. Previous, publicly available empirical research studies using high school grades and college admissions test scores to predict college grades are reviewed, along with research studies on factors affecting Hispanics' college admissions test performance. The report closes with suggestions for further refinement of predictive validity studies of Hispanics' college performance.

The main conclusion to be drawn from this review is that prediction of Hispanics' achievement in college needs to consider the influence of mitigating variables on measures of college aptitude and college achievement. Educational survey data show strong associations between Hispanics' school achievement prior to college and factors related to socioeconomic status, school adjustment, migration-immigration history, and language background. The influences of these factors and others on prediction of Hispanics' college achievement have not been investigated intensively. Publicly available predictive validity studies suggest that the college grades of some U.S. Hispanic students are not predicted as well by high school grades and admissions test scores as are the college grades of nonminority and other Hispanic students. The pattern of results reviewed suggests that a better research understanding is needed for how background, personal factors, and institutional factors affect prediction of Hispanics' college achievement. Finally, in light of the foregoing, there is a need to develop enhanced methods for representing and assessing Hispanics' college achievement, growth or change in achievement, and relation of achievement to background and personal characteristics of students.

The author extends special thanks to ETS and the College Board for support of this report, and for making 1979–80 Hispanic Admissions Testing Program data available for review. Gratitude is also extended to Dr. Jorge Dieppa of the College Board Puerto Rico Office for kindly making available summaries of a number of validity studies that used the Prueba de Aptitud Academica and high school grades to predict Puerto Rican students' college grades. Special thanks are extended to Winton Manning, Michael Olivas, Edward T. Rincon, Stephen Olmedo, Maria Watkins, Luis Laosa, Rose Payán, Mary Jo Clark, Carlos Arce, Jorge Dieppa, Roy Lucero, Donald Alderman, Hunter Breland, and Steven Ivens for serving as commentators on earlier drafts of this report. Thanks are also extended to Sandra MacGowan for editorial assistance and to Jessie Cryer and Margaret Olbrick for careful and efficient preparation of the original manuscript. Finally, thanks are extended to Jerilee Grandy for helpful discussions preceding the planning of this work.

1

Introduction

The purpose of this report is to review issues and previous research surrounding prediction of U.S. Hispanic students' college achievement. The mission of the report is wide in scope, but nonetheless limited in its immediate objectives. Attention is focused only on Hispanics residing in the fifty states and the District of Columbia; unless otherwise indicated, attention is not given to Hispanics residing in Puerto Rico. This report concentrates primarily on summarizing and interpreting selected empirical studies of Hispanics' educational attainment, preparation for college, college aptitude assessment, and prediction of achievement in college. Where feasible, evidence is examined that describes associations between Hispanics' sociocultural and linguistic backgrounds and higher educational preparation or attainment. The ultimate objective of the report is to suggest needed further research, which might improve prediction of Hispanics' college performance.

The report begins with a demographic overview of U.S. Hispanics, concentrating on population size, ethnic subgroup identity, age, economic welfare, language background, and educational attainment. Attention is separately given to variation in Hispanics' demographic characteristics by subgroup membership. The primary sources of information cited in this portion of the review are nationally-based surveys of the general Hispanic populace or of specific Hispanic subpopulations. As appropriate, citations are made to exemplary empirical studies that are not nationally-based but are noteworthy for the questions they investigate, given the absence of broader-based national studies on the same topics. The intent of this first section is to provide the reader with sound, current knowledge of the demographic and educational status of Hispanics in relation to the U.S. population at large. A further goal is to inform the reader in some detail of the extensive diversity that exists across different Hispanic subpopulations in terms of their background characteristics, access to education, and college attainment. The primary Hispanic subpopulations that are discussed include Mexican Americans, Puerto Ricans, and Cuban Americans.

Following the demographic and educational attainment overview of U.S. Hispanics, Chapter 3 briefly surveys the findings of the recent major studies of Hispanics' learning achievement during the high school years. The intent of this portion of the report is not to discuss individual studies in great depth, but rather to concisely summarize the findings of studies in order to provide readers with general information about Hispanics' learning achievement at a point in schooling immediately preceding opportunity for college entrance. This overview is revealing because it outlines many of the obstacles Hispanics face in becoming academically prepared for college. Discussion of the association between Hispanic students' economic, social, and linguistic backgrounds and high school achievement is included in this section, based on findings from national survey studies and other research.

Subsequent to the discussion of high school achievement, Chapter 4 presents characteristics of Hispanics' college admissions test scores based on recent data collected and compiled by the American College Testing Program, the College Entrance Examination Board, and the Graduate Record Examination Board. The first objective of Chapter 4 is to describe admissions test score performance of Hispanics, broken down by Hispanic subgroups where feasible, and further to contrast the level of performance of Hispanics with that of nonethnic minority examinees. A second but limited objective is to inspect evidence of the association between admissions test scores and language characteristics of Hispanic students, as revealed by their responses to questionnaires they were given when they applied to take college admissions tests.

The first part of Chapter 5 is a review of empirical studies evaluating the prediction of undergraduate Hispanics' college grades from high school grades and college admissions test scores. Because publicly available and published studies are limited, most of the research reviewed on Hispanics is concerned primarily with students who are likely Mexican Americans. Also included for discussion are a major series of studies accomplished on Puerto Rican students by the College Board Puerto Rico office, using high school grades and college entrance examination scores as predictors of college grade point average. These latter studies, and one study in Mexico which is discussed, are of interest because they suggest that high school grades and admissions test scores are useful predictors of college performance in a geographical and social context where Hispanic culture and the Spanish language are predominant.

The second part of Chapter 5 reviews selective findings on Hispanics from miscellaneous studies of college aptitude test performance and achievement test performance. The focus of the findings cited is on issues of test bias and the influences of language background and personal characteristics on test performance. Included for review is a small number of studies that specifically investigated the role of proficiency in English as a moderating variable in assessment of Hispanics' college aptitude, based on Spanish or English college aptitude test scores.

Excluded from discussion in Chapter 5 are published works that are nonempirical, primarily conceptual, surveys of factors influencing Hispanics' test performance at large. Such works — e.g., Samuda (1975), Oakland (1977), and DeBlassie (1980) — do not focus on presentation and detailed discussion of empirical evidence regarding Hispanics' college admissions test performances. While these works are excluded from discussion in this report, it should be understood that they ought to serve as useful and valuable references to augment the discussions provided here.

Chapter 6 presents a synthesis of issues underlying improvement in the prediction of Hispanics' college grades and other measures of college success. Discussion is given to the need for broadening the kinds of indicators that might be used to predict either Hispanic students' college aptitude or college achievement. The issues cited are raised in the context of the research reviewed earlier in the report. The last portion of Chapter 6 sketches directions for needed research in the prediction of Hispanics' college achievement. Several broad and specific directions for research are outlined. These directions center on three issues: a) improving understanding of Hispanics' preparation for college; b) improving understanding of how the college admissions process operates for Hispanic candidates; and c) improving understanding of Hispanics' college experiences that affect their college achievement and the prediction of this achievement.

Selective Demographic and Background Overview of U.S. Hispanics: Implications for Educational Attainment

The first major section of this chapter outlines basic information regarding U.S. Hispanics' population size, subpopulation size, income, language characteristics, and educational attainment, as contrasted with the general U.S. population at large. Unless otherwise indicated, only Hispanics residing in the fifty states and the District of Columbia are to be considered. Subsequently, attention is given to differentiation among demographic characteristics of Hispanic subgroups, with an emphasis on educational attainment data. The final section of the chapter discusses language variation among Hispanic subgroups and background factors associated with Hispanic subgroup educational attainment.

CHARACTERISTICS OF THE U.S. HISPANIC POPULATION

Population Size, Age, Income, and Language Background

According to the Bureau of the Census (U.S. Department of Commerce, May 1981), as of March 1980 there were about 13.2 million persons in the United States who were of Spanish origin, excluding Hispanics residing in U.S. territories such as Puerto Rico and U.S. mainland Hispanics who were undocumented immigrants, the latter perhaps numbering up to four million.[1] The figure amounts to approximately six to seven percent of the total U.S. population. Principal Hispanic subgroups in the United States include persons of the following origins: Mexican (7.9 million), Puerto Rican (1.8 million), Cuban (831,000), other Central or South American and Spanish (2.7 million).

As a whole, the U.S. population of Hispanics differs from the general population at large in a number of significant ways pertaining to socioeconomic welfare, age, language background, and educational attainment. In 1978, the median annual income for Hispanic families was $12,566 as compared to $17,912 for non-Hispanic families. The

U.S. Hispanic population is young relative to the remainder of the population, with a median age in 1979 of 22.1 years versus a median age of 30.7 years for non-Hispanics (U.S. Department of Commerce, 1981). According to the Survey of Income and Education (U.S. Department of Health, Education, and Welfare, NCES, 1978b), three out of four U.S. Hispanics were born in the United States.[2] Overall, four out of five U.S. Hispanics lived in Spanish-speaking households, and one out of three Hispanics usually spoke Spanish. In 1976, only about 14 percent of U.S. Hispanics reported an English-only language background (op cit).

Educational Attainment, Income, and Language Background

The most current and comprehensive national overview of educational characteristics of U.S. Hispanics is provided by the report, *The Condition of Education for Hispanic Americans* (U.S. Department of Education, NCES, 1980). This report, abbreviated *CEH, 1980,* is the principal summary source of Hispanic education survey data reviewed here.

Educational attainment among Hispanics lags far behind that of the population as a whole at all levels of schooling. In 1977, only 55.5 percent of Hispanics aged 18 to 34 years had completed high school, as compared to 83.9 percent of white persons of the same age range (*CEH, 1980,* pp. 138–139). Detailed findings examining contrasts between Hispanics' and white non-Hispanics' schooling achievement prior to college are discussed in the next chapter.

In 1977, college enrollment estimates (*CEH, 1980,* pp. 138–139) showed that among high school graduates aged 18 to 34 years, Hispanics had a college enrollment rate of 21.2 percent, as compared to 19.8 percent for the population at large. The apparent parity in college enrollment rates for Hispanic high school graduates and high school graduates at large is subject to different interpretations. First, assuming high school graduation is a requirement for college admissions, then the gross figures indicate a parity in college enrollment rates for Hispanics and non-Hispanics who graduate from high school. The college enrollment rates cited, however, do not support parity in college admissions for Hispanic and non-Hispanic populations at large, since proportionally fewer Hispanics graduate from high school than non-Hispanics. Finally to complicate matters further, Hispanics tend to graduate from high school at a later age than non-Hispanics due to a variety of factors. Hence among persons 18 to 34 years of age who are still in high school, more Hispanics than non-Hispanics do not graduate from high school and do not go on to college.

Table 1

Percent of Hispanic and White Populations Aged 18 to 34, by Education Status and College Enrollment: 1972–77

Year	Hispanic	White[1]
	Enrollment in college as percent of the 18 to 34 population	
1972	8.3	16.0
1973	10.3	15.2
1974	11.5	15.7
1975	12.7	16.8
1976	14.2	16.6
1977	11.8	16.6
	Enrollment in college as percent of high school graduates in the 18 to 34 population	
1972	16.9	19.9
1973	20.4	18.6
1974	21.9	19.0
1975	22.9	20.1
1976	22.8	20.0
1977	21.2	19.8
	High school graduates as a percent of the 18 to 34 population	
1972	49.5	80.4
1973	50.5	81.8
1974	52.6	82.7
1975	55.3	83.4
1976	53.3	83.0
1977	55.5	83.9

[1] Includes white Hispanics.

SOURCE: U.S. Department of Commerce, Bureau of the Census, *Social and Economic Characteristics of Students, October 1972–October 1977.* Current Population Reports, Series P-20, and unpublished tabulations, as cited in U.S. Department of Education, National Center for Education Statistics, *The Condition of Education for Hispanic Americans.* Compiled and edited by G. H. Brown, N. Rosen, and M. A. Olivas. Washington, D.C.: 1980, p. 138.

Figure 1

College Enrollment as Percent of the 18- to 34-year-old Population, for Hispanics

The rate of enrollment in college among Hispanics 18 to 34 years old increased from 1972 to 1977, but never reached the same rate as that for whites.

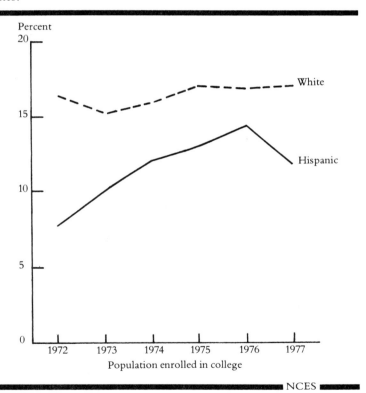

SOURCE: U.S. Department of Education, National Center for Education Statistics, *The Condition of Education for Hispanic Americans.* Compiled and edited by G. H. Brown, N. Rosen, and M. A. Olivas. Washington, D.C.: 1980, p. 139.

The college enrollment statistics cited from the Bureau of the Census (*CEH, 1980*, pp. 138–139) also present data on change in college enrollment rates among Hispanics and whites for the period 1972 through 1977. Over this period, the data show that Hispanics' college enrollment for the age range of 18 to 34 years increased from a low of 8.3 percent in 1972 to a high of 14.2 percent in 1976; thereafter, enrollment was followed by a decline in 1977 to 11.8 percent. Table 1 and Figure 1 (*CEH, 1980*) summarize the information discussed on college enrollment rates of Hispanics and whites in the age range 18 to 34 years for the period from 1972 to 1977.

Data given in the *CEH, 1980* report (p. 148) for fall 1978 show that 42 percent of all Hispanic part-time and full-time college students were concentrated in two-year colleges, while only 23 percent of white non-Hispanic part-time and full-time college students attended two-year colleges. These data suggest the very real possibility that gross numerical increases in college enrollment rates for Hispanics may be occurring most drastically in terms of increased Hispanic two-year college attendance. This hypothesis needs empirical investigation.

Table 2 and Figure 2 (*CEH, 1980*, pp. 146–147) display 1978 full-time undergraduate college enrollment figures for Hispanics and

Table 2

Percent of Hispanic and White Undergraduates Who Attended Institutions of Higher Education Full-time,[1] by Type of Institution: Fall 1978

Type of institution	Hispanic	White, non-Hispanic
Total	57	68
Two-year college	37	35
Four-year institutions, total	77	83
Universities	85	87
Other four-year colleges	75	80

[1] Those whose academic load-coursework or other required activity is at least 75 percent of the full-time load.

SOURCE: U.S. Department of Health, Education, and Welfare, National Center for Education Statistics, Opening Fall Enrollment, 1978, special tabulations, as cited in U.S. Department of Education, National Center for Education Statistics, *The Condition of Education for Hispanic Americans.* Compiled and edited by G. H. Brown, N. Rosen, and M. A. Olivas. Washington, D.C.: 1980, p. 146.

Figure 2

Percent of Hispanic and White Full-time Undergraduates, by Type of Institution

A third of both Hispanics and whites in
two-year colleges were
full-time students. In
universities and other
four-year colleges, a
lower percent of Hispanics than whites
attended full-time.

**Type of
institution**

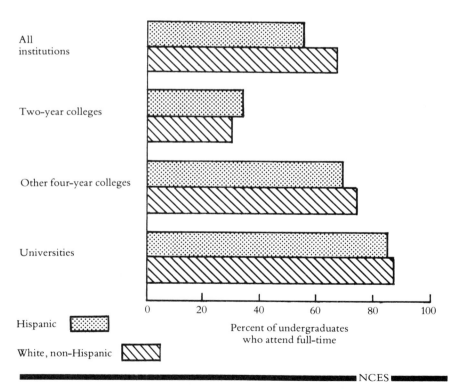

SOURCE: U.S. Department of Education, National Center for Education Statistics, *The Condition of Education for Hispanic Americans.* Compiled and edited by G. H. Brown, N. Rosen, and
M. A. Olivas. Washington, D.C.: 1980, p. 147.

whites. For those high school graduates who went on to college, the percentage of Hispanic students who assumed full-time study in 1978 was 57 percent, as compared to 68 percent for white non-Hispanic youths. According to these statistics, Hispanics thus show about a ten percent lower full-time college attendance rate. Closer examination of the data shows that the difference in full-time attendance rates for Hispanics and white non-Hispanics is greatest in four-year colleges rather than two-year colleges.

Once in college, fewer proportions of Hispanics than white non-Hispanics tend to select major areas of study related to high levels of professional aspiration. For example, 1978 survey data cited in the *CEH, 1980* report (pp. 170–171) indicate that proportionately fewer Hispanics than white non-Hispanic undergraduates were enrolled in the biological sciences, business and management, engineering, and the physical sciences.

Other marked contrasts in college enrollment patterns between Hispanic and non-Hispanic students are revealed in the institutions that each group selected for enrollment and the geographical locale of such institutions. According to the *CEH, 1980* report (pp. 118–119), Hispanics tend to attend institutions in centers of Hispanic population, such as in the Southwest and major urban centers in the East. Twenty-one two-year and four-year institutions accounted for 24 percent of all Hispanics enrolled in college in 1978 (*CEH, 1980*, p. 119). Four-year institutions that many Hispanics enrolled in have been characterized as "less prestigious" than other four-year institutions (Rincon, personal note).

Further detailed demographic information regarding Hispanics' college enrollment characteristics and the institutional characteristics and location of colleges selected by Hispanics are to be found in the following volumes: *Access to College for Mexican Americans in the Southwest* (Ferrin, Jonsen, and Trimble, 1972); *Chicanos in Higher Education: Status and Issues* (Lopez, Madrid-Barela, and Macias, 1976); *Minorities in Higher Education: Chicanos and Others* (Cabrera, 1978); *The Dilemma of Access* (Olivas, 1979); and *Mexican-American/Chicano Students in Institutions of Higher Education: Access, Attrition, and Achievement* (de los Santos, Jr., Montemayor, and Solis, Jr., 1980).

Table 3 and Figure 3 (*CEH, 1980*, pp. 188–189) contrast the rate of college attendance in 1976 for Hispanic and non-Hispanic students who graduated from high school in 1972. Other data from the National Longitudinal Study of the High School Class of 1972 (*CEH, 1980*, pp. 182–183) show that college attendance rates in October 1972 for students in the graduating class of 1972 were 85.9 percent for white

Table 3

Educational Status as of October 1976 of Hispanics and Whites in the High School Class of 1972 Who Enrolled in Academic Programs in Fall 1972, by Sex

	Hispanic		White, non-Hispanic	
Educational status	**Men**	**Women**	**Men**	**Women**
	(Percent distribution)			
Total	100	100	100	100
Bachelor's degree	14	18	36	46
No degree, but still enrolled	29	28	30	20
Dropouts	57	54	34	34
Number of respondents	137	113	3,352	2,892

SOURCE: U.S. Department of Health, Education, and Welfare, National Center for Education Statistics, National Longitudinal Survey of the High School Class of 1972. *A Capsule Description of Young Adults Four and One-Half Years After High School,* by Bruce Eckland and Joseph Wisenbaker, February 1979, as cited in U.S. Department of Education, National Center for Education Statistics, *The Condition of Education for Hispanic Americans.* Compiled and edited by G. H. Brown, N. Rosen, and M. A. Olivas. Washington, D.C.: 1980, p. 188.

non-Hispanics and 78.5 percent for Hispanics. By 1976, four years after high school graduation, approximately 55 percent of Hispanics who had gone on to college had dropped out before obtaining a bachelor's degree. In contrast, only 34 percent of the white non-Hispanic student cohort had left college. The impact of attrition is also revealed in graduation rates, which showed that two and one-half times as many white non-Hispanics as Hispanics had obtained their bachelor's degree after four years of college enrollment.

Data from the Survey of Income and Education summarized in the *CEH, 1980* report (pp. 194–195) reveal that 47 percent of Hispanic college students who were financially dependent on their parents in spring 1976 came from families with an annual income of less than $10,000. This figure is in contrast to 20 percent of college students overall who were financially dependent on parents earning less than $10,000 annually. Other data (*CEH, 1980,* pp. 196–197) reveal that, in spring 1976, 53 percent of all Hispanic college students' families had a head of household who had not completed high school; this figure contrasts

Figure 3

Educational Status of Hispanics and Whites Four Years after Entering College

Four years after enroll-
ing in academic pro-
grams, two-and-one-
half times as many
white women and men
had a bachelor's degree
as their Hispanic
counterparts.

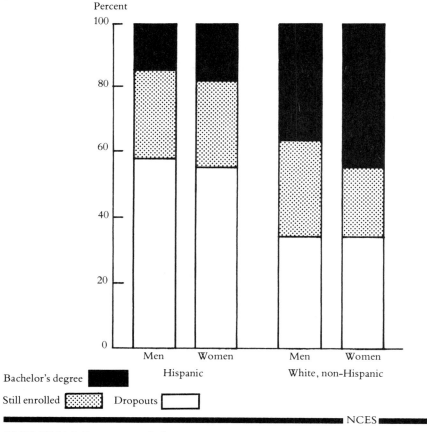

SOURCE: U.S. Department of Education, National Center for Education Statistics, *The Condition of Education for Hispanic Americans.* Compiled and edited by G. H. Brown, N. Rosen, and
M. A. Olivas. Washington, D.C.: 1980, p. 189.

with a rate of 15 percent for white non-Hispanics. Fifty-four percent of heads of households of white non-Hispanic college students had attended some college or were college graduates, compared with 26 percent of heads of households of Hispanic college students.

Interestingly, "financial difficulties" have been cited more often by Hispanic students than by white non-Hispanic students as a major factor influencing withdrawal from college. This point is apparent in Table 4 and Figure 4 (*CEH, 1980*, pp. 184–185), which present data on reasons given by Hispanics and white non-Hispanics for college withdrawal. These data show that Hispanics and white non-Hispanics gave similar reasons for their withdrawal from college. In the study generating these data however, white non-Hispanics were noticeably more likely to drop out of college than Hispanics due to a belief that schoolwork was not relevant to real world circumstances.

The aggregate effects of the problems that Hispanics face in completing a college education are demonstrated by the low proportion of Hispanics who receive college degrees relative to the number of college degrees conferred. For example, in the period 1976–77, U.S. mainland Hispanics earned 4.1 percent of all associate degrees from two-year colleges, and 2 percent or less of all bachelor's, master's, and Ph.D. degrees conferred (*CEH, 1980*, pp. 164–165). The significance of this data is emphasized by recalling that 6 to 7 percent of the total population is Hispanic.

Attention is now given to the general language background of Hispanics in relation to educational access and attainment issues. The association between Hispanics' language background and educational attainment has only been investigated sporadically in national survey research. In a summary of 1976 data drawn from the Survey of Income and Education, the National Center for Education Statistics (U.S. Department of Health, Education, and Welfare, NCES, 1978a) reported a positive association between Hispanics' recidivism in elementary and high school grades and non-English-language background. The relevant summary of data is reproduced in Table 5. The association of language background with recidivism is most marked for Hispanic students enrolled in grades 5 through 12. For the grade range 5 through 8, Hispanic students with a non-English-language background were roughly 4 times as likely to be behind the grade level expected for their ages than were Hispanic students with an English-language background. For the grade range 9 through 12, Hispanics with a non-English background were 1.5 times as likely to be behind expected grade level than were Hispanics with an English-language background.

Table 4

Reasons Given by Hispanics and Whites in the High School Class of 1972 for Withdrawing by October 1973 from the Postsecondary School Attended in October 1972

Reasons	Percent answering "applies to me":	
	Hispanic	White, non-Hispanic
Had financial difficulties	32	23
Wanted to get practical experience	26	27
Failed, or not doing as well as wanted	26	21
Offered a good job	18	19
Marriage or marriage plans	16	15
School work not relevant to real world	7	19
Family emergency	7	3
Other (illness, etc.)	2	6

NOTE: More than one answer could be chosen if applicable.

SOURCE: U.S. Department of Health, Education, and Welfare, National Center for Education Statistics, National Longitudinal Study of the High School Class of 1972, *Comparative Profiles One and One-half Years After Graduation,* as cited in U.S. Department of Education, National Center for Education Statistics, *The Condition of Education for Hispanic Americans.* Compiled and edited by G. H. Brown, N. Rosen, and M. A. Olivas. Washington, D.C.: 1980, p. 184.

The rate of recidivism was about 2 to 3 times as high for Hispanic students who reported usual reliance on a non-English language (presumably Spanish) than the rate of recidivism for Hispanics who reported usual reliance on English. Care needs to be taken in interpreting the findings discussed because the association between recidivism and language background is undoubtedly confounded with other background characteristics of Hispanics and with the quality of schooling services provided to Hispanics who are more likely to speak Spanish.

According to the *CEH, 1980* report data (pp. 200–201), a distinguishing characteristic of U.S. Hispanic college students is their language background and opportunity for bilingualism. Overall in 1976, 81 percent of Hispanic college students were estimated to come from non-English speaking backgrounds where, presumably Spanish was

Figure 4

Reasons Given by Hispanics and Whites for Withdrawing by October 1973 from the Postsecondary School Attended in October 1972

Financial difficulties was the reason most often cited by Hispanics for withdrawing from postsecondary education. In contrast, whites most often withdrew to obtain practical experience.

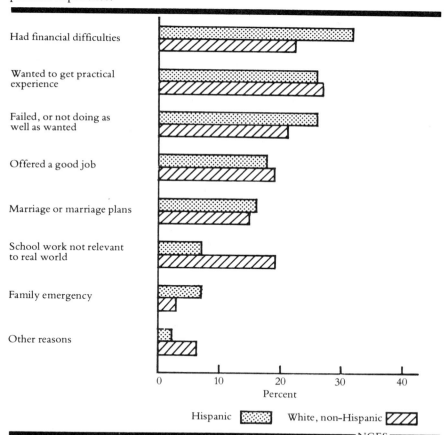

SOURCE: U.S. Department of Education, National Center for Education Statistics, *The Condition of Education for Hispanic Americans.* Compiled and edited by G. H. Brown, N. Rosen and M. A. Olivas. Washington, D.C.: 1980, p. 185.

Table 5

Numbers and Percentages of Students Age 6 to 20 in Grades 1 to 12 Who Were Below Expected Grade Levels,[1] **by Totals, Ethnic Origin, and Language Characteristics: Spring 1976**
(Numbers in thousands)

Ethnic origin and grade level of students aged 6 to 20 enrolled in grades 1 to 12	Total	English-language back-ground	Non-English-language background			
				Usual individual language		
			Total	English	Non-English	Not reported
Students of Hispanic origin						
Total	3,050	548	2,493	1,748	563	182
Below expected grade	394	36	357	199	138	20
Percent	(13)	(7)	(14)	(11)	(25)	(11)
In grades 1 to 4	1,104	225	876	568	246	63
Below expected grade	88	13	75	34	36	4
Percent	(8)	(6)	(9)	(6)	(15)	(7)
In grades 5 to 8	1,171	202	965	700	191	74
Below expected grade	158	8	151	81	61	10
Percent	(14)	(4)	(16)	(12)	(32)	(13)
In grades 9 to 12	774	122	652	480	126	45
Below expected grade	148	16	132	84	41	6
Percent	(19)	(13)	(20)	(18)	(33)	(14)

[1] Eight years old or older in the first grade, nine years old or older in the second grade, etc.

SOURCE: U.S. Department of Health, Education, and Welfare, 1978a.

the alternative language. Only 30 percent of Hispanic college students surveyed reported either that they were from a totally mono-English background or that they did not speak a non-English language despite being from a household where a non-English language was spoken. Fully 67 percent of Hispanic college students surveyed reported frequent or occasional use of a non-English language. Further discussion on the relationship of language characteristics to Hispanic subgroup membership, immigration history, and educational attainment is presented later in this and other chapters in the present report.

HISPANIC SUBPOPULATION CHARACTERISTICS

Subpopulation Size, Age, and Language Background

Comprehending factors that affect Hispanics' access to college and ultimate achievement in college first requires sensitivity to variation in the background of Hispanics. While U.S. Hispanics differ noticeably from white non-Hispanics in terms of immigration history, age, income, and language background, there exists considerable diversity among Hispanics, which is associated with Hispanic subgroup membership. In this section, an overview of selected demographic characteristics is presented for three major Hispanic groups: Mexican Americans, Mainland Puerto Ricans, and Cuban Americans.

In 1976, of an estimated 11.2 million Hispanic persons in the United States, three out of four were born on the mainland or in Puerto Rico (U.S. Department of Health, Education, and Welfare, 1978b). Only 21 percent of Mexican Americans were born in Mexico or in another foreign country, while half of the mainland Puerto Rican populace was born in Puerto Rico. Cuban Americans showed the highest birthrate outside of the United States, with 80 percent of such persons born abroad (almost all in Cuba).

As of March 1980, an estimated 28.4 percent of the non-Hispanic U.S. population was under 18 years of age in contrast to 29.8 percent of the Cuban American population, 44.3 percent of the U.S. Puerto Rican population, and 42.4 percent of the Mexican American population (U.S. Department of Commerce, 1981). Economically, the estimated median income of Cuban American families in March of 1980 was $17,538, in contrast to estimated median incomes of $15,171 for Mexican American families, $9,855 for Puerto Rican families, $15,470 for other Hispanic families, and $19,965 for non-Hispanic families (op cit). Proportionally more Cuban Americans (49.1 percent) over the age of 25 in 1978 were estimated to have completed high school than Mexican Americans (34.3 percent) or U.S. Puerto Ricans (36 percent), but these figures were still far below those (67.1 percent) for the U.S. non-Hispanic populace over the age of 25 (*CEH, 1980*, pp. 22–23). Among persons 25 years or older in 1979, 13.9 percent of Cuban Americans were estimated to have completed at least four years of college in comparison to 4.3 percent of Mexican Americans, 4.2 percent of Puerto Ricans, and 13.8 percent of other Hispanics, these figures contrasting with 16.1 percent of the U.S. non-Hispanic population (op cit).

Consideration is now turned to differences in language background found among Hispanic subgroups according to level of education attainment. No published analyses of national survey data of such language background differences by educational attainment level for grade school and high school children of different Hispanic subgroups were encountered as of the date of this report. The analysis of Survey of Income and Education data discussed earlier (U.S. Department of Health, Education, and Welfare, 1978a) does not include the requisite breakdown by Hispanic subgroup membership for either the ranges of age or education levels in question.

Recent data on language usage at home among members of different Hispanic subgroups enrolled as sophomores and seniors in high school in 1980 are found in Nielson and Fernandez (1981). This study of Hispanic students, sampled randomly from the U.S. population of high school students, found that Cuban-origin sophomores and senior students showed the strongest preponderance of Spanish usage at home, with Puerto Rican and Mexican American students following in that order.

Table 6 (*CEH, 1980*, p. 200) shows some noteworthy language background differences among Hispanic college students according to Hispanic subgroup identity. Ninety-nine percent of Cuban American college students in 1976 were estimated to come from non-English speaking backgrounds, in contrast to 84 percent of Puerto Rican and 84 percent of Mexican American college students. Mexican American college students reported the lowest current usage of Spanish, with 66 percent estimated to be frequent or occasional speakers of the language. A similar figure, 70 percent, is reported for Puerto Rican college students, but a much higher figure, 96 percent, is reported for Cuban American college students. Overall, these data support the conclusion that significant numbers of college students from each of the Hispanic subgroups have a continuing, intensive exposure to the Spanish language extending beyond the years of primary and secondary schooling.

Table 6

Distribution of Hispanic College Students,[1] by Language Characteristics and by Subgroup: Spring 1976

Language characteristics	Total Hispanics	Hispanic subgroup			
		Mexican American	Puerto Rican	Cuban	Other Hispanics
Total	100	100	100	100	100
Mono-English-language background[2]	19	16	*	*	32
Non-English-language background[3]	81	84	84	99	68
Speak only English themselves[4]	11	13	*	*	*
Speak a non-English language themselves[5]	67	66	70	96	58
Not reported	*	*	*	*	*

* Percent not shown where base is less than 20,000 persons.
[1] Enrolled in college at any level. Excludes Puerto Rico and outlying territories.
[2] English was the only language spoken in the household as a child and is the only language spoken in the household currently.
[3] A non-English language was spoken in the household as a child and/or is spoken (either sometimes or usually) in the household currently.
[4] Although from a non-English-language background, the individual only speaks English.
[5] The individual speaks a non-English language either sometimes or usually.
NOTE: Details may not add to totals because of rounding.

SOURCE: U.S. Department of Health, Education, and Welfare, National Center for Education Statistics, Survey of Income and Education, Spring 1976, special tabulations, as cited in U.S. Department of Education, National Center for Education Statistics, *The Condition of Education for Hispanic Americans.* Compiled and edited by G. H. Brown, N. Rosen, and M. A. Olivas. Washington, D.C.: 1980, p. 200.

It is important to understand that frequency of use of Spanish or English among Hispanics is not a simply understood variable in terms of its potential association with schooling performance. The next section offers an overview of sociolinguistic and other background characteristics that are associated with Hispanic subgroup members' educational attainment.

Hispanics' Subgroup Language Variation, Background, and Educational Attainment

This section focuses in more detail on some general language background characteristics of Hispanic subgroups that are of known or potential relevance to educational attainment. The issues discussed are intended to highlight some important characteristics of language background that are relevant to Hispanics' educational attainment. No exhaustive or highly systematic treatment of issues is intended. The next chapter discusses language proficiency factors and cultural interactional norms that possibly affect learning in Hispanics during high school; it also discusses other significant factors that affect Hispanics' high school achievement. The present section is a broadly conceived, descriptive overview of Hispanics' language characteristics, broken down by Hispanic subgroup and social background. Issues of educational attainment are included where pertinent.

Mexican Americans' language background in Spanish and English is distinguished from other Hispanic subgroups' background by several features that have a potential impact on schooling. First, number of generations removed from Mexico and geographical distance in the United States from the Mexican border tend to be negatively associated with ability to speak Spanish but positively associated with ability to speak English. There are exceptions to the influence of geographical distance from Mexico, such as is the case with Midwest cities (e.g., Chicago) where there are high rates of immigration on the part of immigrants from Mexico who are Spanish dominant. Another exception to the influence of geographical distance from Mexico on use of Spanish is the case of northern New Mexico, where descendants of the original Spanish explorers of the Americas have spoken Spanish primarily since 1598. Spanish is spoken more frequently among Hispanics in parts of northern New Mexico than it is spoken by some Hispanics to the south of that area within the United States.

A recent dissertation by Macias (1979), *Mexican/Chicano Sociolinguistic Behavior and Language Policy in the United States*, presents perhaps the most thorough synthesis to date of existing language survey data on Mexican Americans and other Hispanic subgroups. The Macias work is also noteworthy in that it represents the most thorough, currently available analysis of responses of Mexican Americans to language items on the Survey of Income and Education of 1976 (SIE, 1976). Some significant trends in the Macias synthesis of Mexican American language background based on the Survey of Income and Education data of 1976 are presented below.

According to Macias (1979, p. 50), "Only around 14.1 percent of the Mexican-origin population is of English-language background (lives in an exclusively English household, and — if over 14 years of age — has an English mother tongue)." Overall, Mexican American respondents in the SIE, 1976, survey reported slightly more frequent (i.e., "usual") reliance on Spanish than English; also, they reported Spanish more often overall than English as a second language. More than 75 percent of Mexican Americans over 14 years of age reported that Spanish was their mother tongue; here the term *mother tongue* refers to the language spoken in respondents' households when they were children and not necessarily the language spoken at home by respondents. Among SIE, 1976, Mexican American respondents above 14 years of age, Macias found that: a) 9.6 percent of the respondents spoke only English; b) 35.7 percent spoke English as their usual language and Spanish as their second language; c) 17.9 percent spoke only Spanish; and d) 22 percent spoke Spanish as their usual language and English as their second language. The SIE, 1976, survey results that are cited suggest that adult Mexican Americans maintain strong patterns of contact with both the English and Spanish languages.

A 1979 demographic study of Mexican Americans by Arce (cited in *La Red*, 1981) involved a national probability sample of 1,000 Mexican American households and included questionnaire or interview items on language use. In this study, adult respondents judged themselves to be more fluent in conversation in Spanish than conversation in English. The Arce data also supported the finding that Mexican American respondents were likely to be *spoken to* in Spanish by their parents or elders, but were more likely to use English on occasion in *speaking to* their parents, with Spanish still being maintained as the prime common language of communication between parents and children. In turn, spouses, who presumably were not elders, were found to rely more on English than on Spanish in their mutual communications with each other. These spouses relied even more frequently on English in their communication with children.

In a comparative study of Mexican American, Puerto Rican, and Cuban American use of Spanish and English, Laosa (1975, p. 622) found overall that frequent use of English by central Texas Mexican American parents was associated with even more frequent use of English by the children of those parents. The parts of the Laosa (1975) study that deal with Mexican Americans also found that parents who used English as the most frequent home language tended to have children who spoke mainly English at home. Parents who spoke Spanish at home most frequently tended to have children who most frequently spoke an intermixed variety of Spanish and English at home. Parents who most frequently spoke either Spanish or English at home, but not an intermixture of the two languages at home, had children who tended to rely most frequently on the same pattern of separated language use at home. Finally, within the above context of results, parents who spoke an intermixed variety of Spanish and English as the most frequent pattern had children who tended to speak primarily English at home. The Laosa study also found that Mexican American children were more likely to use English than Spanish in non-home settings such as school or community. The results Laosa obtained for his Mexican American sample strongly suggest that there was increased reliance on English and less reliance on Spanish as parents tended to use more English. Even when Mexican American parents tended not to speak English at home, the children of those parents tended to speak some English at home. Further reference will be made to the Laosa (1975) study in forthcoming sections on language use patterns of mainland Puerto Ricans and Cuban Americans.

The results of the Macias (1977) study, the study cited in *La Red* (1981), and the Laosa (1975) study strongly suggest that there are intergenerational factors that affect preference for using Spanish and English. The results suggest the hypothesis that there is more use of English by Mexican American children than by their parents and that this effect increases from generation to generation.

As exposure to English increases among Mexican Americans, maintenance of ability to speak Spanish has not been widely addressed in the demographic survey literature. In reviewing relevant issues and studies, Hernández-Chávez (1978, pp. 527–528) concluded:

> There is a growing body of evidence that demonstrates that Spanish-speaking communities are shifting dramatically to English. In general, studies of language use are beginning to show very clearly that third generation Mexican Americans — and in urban areas even second generation speakers — are following the familiar pattern of other non-English languages in the United States. The first generation acquires a limited amount of English in adulthood, the second generation becomes bilingual, and the third generation shifts to English.
>
> On the other hand, census studies show a steady increase in the number of Spanish speakers, due mostly to a continued high rate of immigration. We have the paradoxical situation, then, where Spanish-speaking communities in the United States are rapidly losing their ethnic tongue even though Spanish, as a language, enjoys perhaps the greatest number of speakers of a non-English language in the history of the country.

It is important to understand that the views of Hernández-Chávez described above do not constitute more than a hypothesis about what may be occurring among Mexican Americans with regard to their linguistic assimilation into the English language. The demographic growth characteristics of Mexican Americans in urban areas such as Los Angeles, for example, may lead to widespread social circumstances where Spanish is actively displacing English as the most necessary language for daily life and commerce within certain major urban neighborhoods and shopping areas. Thus, there may be a possibility that under some existing U.S. social circumstances furthered growth in the use of Spanish occurs. Hernández-Chávez (1978) indicated that maintenance of Spanish is a function of frequency of Spanish use in community settings of everyday importance. At this point in time, there do not appear to exist any research studies on Mexican Americans that investigate circumstances under which there is a reversal of the generational trend of Mexican American individuals to lose Spanish.

Attention is now briefly turned to sociolinguistic research on linguistic characteristics of Mexican Americans' English and Spanish. The major question posed in this research has been how the sound-structure, word-structure, grammar, and interlingual mixture of languages are related to the social background of Mexican Americans. For systematic surveys of this area, the reader is referred to Peñalosa (1981) and Teschner, Bills, and Cradock (1975).

Investigations of the English spoken by Mexican Americans suggest that it may show characteristics related to knowledge of Spanish and that Mexican Americans' social background and exposure to Spanish is an important factor underlying these influences. Evidence of Spanish influence on the English of Mexican Americans is given by pronunciation of vowels in English words—for example, pronouncing the "i" in "pin" by the sound "ea" corresponding to the Spanish sound for the letter "i." Other characteristics of Mexican American English may show formation of inappropriate grammatical structure in English —for example, "How many years do you have?" in attempting to formulate a meaningful statement for the appropriate English equivalent, "How old are you?" The foregoing examples are given just to illustrate some of the kinds of phenomena that arise in the English of Mexican Americans who have extensive Spanish-language background. Of course, the range of examples that could be given is considerably more complex and extensive and includes issues of nonequivalent meanings of words, expressions, and idioms across Spanish and English. The point to be made about the kinds of phenomena just cited is that while they may be considered to show lack of English proficiency, they also have been found to occur as socially stable, acceptable, and functional versions of English in some Hispanic community settings. While there is no question that lack of proficiency in standard English may impede educational access in the United States, there still remains the fact that some Mexican Americans are exposed to varieties of English that are nonstandard but nonetheless acceptable in many everyday social contexts in which Mexican Americans or Hispanics communicate among each other or with non-Hispanics familiar with such varieties.

A corollary to the above point is that apparent errors in the English speech of Mexican Americans may emanate not only from unfamiliarity with standard English but also from knowledge of socially accepted variants of standard English.

Investigations of the written English of Mexican Americans have not been extensive. One excellent source for sociolinguistic research in this area is in papers found in the volume, *College, English, and the Mexican American* (Willcott and Ornstein, 1977). A second excellent source of information is in selected papers comprising the proceedings of a 1981 conference on Chicano English organized by Jacob Ornstein-Galicia.[3] Written English of Mexican Americans may show different levels of Spanish influence, as is the case with spoken English. At the level of spelling (orthography), there is the possibility that nonstandard conventions for pronouncing English words may lead to misspelling of words — for example, the pronunciation "seating" for the English word "sitting." Other kinds of English spelling errors may arise in attempts to spell an English word on the basis of a spelling of the same word in its Spanish version — for example, "comfort" as "confort," like the Spanish "confortable" (Herrick, 1981). At the grammatical level, errors such as use of double negatives in English may reflect valid use of such negatives in Spanish syntax. Other common grammatical errors involve malformation of past tense and past participles of verbs, lack of subject-verb agreement, and omission of articles, etc. Some of these sorts of errors in English writing are easy to ascribe to knowledge of Spanish, while other sorts of errors more likely reflect familiarity with spoken English coupled with low familiarity with written English.

Investigation of higher-level discourse organization of Mexican American high school students' English essays has found evidence of poor writing that is attributable to lack of training in writing (Janice Randle, St. Edwards University, personal note). When they do occur, errors of this class are exhibited by poor organization of essay contents, fragmented expression of ideas, inconsistent style, and misuse of common words, for example. While some of these higher-level errors in Mexican Americans' English language essays might be attributable to knowledge of Spanish, these errors taken as a whole reflect poor writing skills that are more likely attributable to opportunities to learn writing skills in school. A research study touching on Hispanic college candidates' writing skills by Breland and Griswold (1982) is discussed later in this report.

Attention is now turned to sociolinguistic studies of Mexican Americans' Spanish. Researchers have found that there is no single variety of spoken Spanish in contrast to a more or less common international form of standard written Spanish. Spoken Mexican American Spanish has been estimated to have distinctive dialects in northern New Mexico and Arizona, in addition to a general Southwest Spanish dialect drawing from the spoken Spanish of northern Mexico (Ornstein-Galicia, 1981). Conversational uses of some varieties of U. S. Spanish often involve borrowing of words from English to achieve special communicative effects. To be sure, variations among these forms of spoken Spanish are minor, but the implications for education (e.g., bilingual programs) are far from trivial in terms of setting standards for oral Spanish proficiency in classroom settings. Aguirre (1980) has found that preference for speaking Spanish in place of English was a marker for adolescents' "Chicano" identity in U.S.-Mexico border communities. Thus, in preference for languages, there are social identity issues raised along with implications for instruction.

Yet another complication in understanding characteristics of Mexican American Spanish is the existence of Pachuco (youth cult) argot Spanish and varieties of intermixed Spanish and English known popularly, but often derogatorily, as "Tex Mex" or "Spanglish." Use of these codes or varieties of Spanish is often socially expected and appropriate in social settings among Mexican Americans near U.S. border areas or in major Southwest urban barrio settings. Sociolinguistic analyses of these codes reveals that speakers evidence a good understanding and command of syntax and word formation rules based on "standard" Spanish and English. For example, the English verb "to type" becomes integrated into Spanish as the verb "taypear" and is used henceforth in accordance with Spanish syntax (Reyes, 1981).

The impact and presence of bilingual education on Mexican Americans' language capabilities is as yet unclear due to the difficulties of carrying out programs and appraising their effects on educational outcomes. For a review of issues and research pointing to the success of bilingual programs, see Troike (1980). Results of anecdotal observation and actual research suggest that in some cases immigrant Mexican children who have been schooled entirely in Spanish in Mexico, and who come from middle-class Mexican backgrounds, eventually outperform Mexican American children in primary grades taught entirely in English in the United States. However, some research has found just the opposite with Mexican immigrant children of lower socio-economic backgrounds (Baral, 1979). Baral's survey of previous find-ings and his own work support Cummins' (1980) conclusions that intensive primary schooling in a home language in a bilingual school-ing context spanning several years is often necessary in order to sup-port the development of cognitive skills necessary for school achieve-ment in English. The fact that in English language classes Mexican Americans with English as a home language rather than Spanish may outperform Mexican Americans with a home background in Spanish could be due in no small part to the similarity of language experiences in English across home-school settings for those with English language backgrounds. It may be that the literacy characteristics of *home and community* language experiences outside of school are critical; this view is supported by findings of Canadian research showing that mid-dle-class Anglophone students immersed in French language class-rooms have been found to transfer knowledge learned in French into English language expositions of this knowledge. Presumably such Anglophone students are learning how to read and write in English — a socially prestigious language — outside of school.

More detailed discussion of classroom implications of language use and cultural norms for communication among Mexican Americans and other Hispanics is given in the next section. Attention is now turned to important language variation characteristics of Puerto Ricans.

The language history of Puerto Ricans is a complex subject. In 1898, Spanish was the only official language of the Island of Puerto Rico. Following United States takeover of the Island at the culmina-tion of the Spanish-American War, English was introduced in the schooling of Puerto Ricans, most often in concert with use of Spanish for instruction of certain subject areas and school grades. Spanish as the sole language of instruction was not reintroduced into the public school system until 1948, at which time instruction in English as a second language was mandated in grades beginning with the first (von Maltitz, 1975). Regardless of where they were born — mainland United States or Puerto Rico — over 90 percent of U.S. Puerto Ricans are presently estimated to have Spanish as the native language (U.S. Department of Health, Education, and Welfare, NCES, 1978b).

According to Aspira of America (1976), in 1970 approximately 98 percent of U.S. mainland Puerto Ricans lived in large metropolitan areas, as compared with 70 percent for the U.S. population as a whole. According to Aspira, major urban concentrations of Puerto Ricans occurred in urban clusters adjoining the New York City-New Jersey-Pennsylvania area; Chicago; Hartford, Connecticut; Buffalo and Rochester, New York; New York City; Cleveland; Boston; Los Angeles; and San Francisco.

No detailed demographic report of language characteristics of U.S. Puerto Ricans on a national scale exists that would be comparable to Macias' (1979) work on Mexican Americans based on the Survey of Income and Education data. However, the potential for such a report exists in the data base collected as part of the Survey of Income and Education of 1976. Sociolinguistic surveys and studies of Puerto Ricans have been conducted in New York City by Fishman, et al. (1971) and Wolfram (1972), and are in progress by the Language Policy Task Force, Center for Puerto Rican Studies, City University of New York.

The research efforts of the Center for Puerto Rican Studies have been concentrated in "el barrio" East Harlem, New York City — one of the oldest, if not the oldest, continuous Puerto Rican community on the mainland (Attinasi, 1979, and Language Policy Task Force, 1980). The findings of sociolinguistic research in "el barrio," while often based only on a relatively small number of subjects (e.g., under 100 respondents in Attinasi, 1979), have suggested that preference for Spanish vs. English and proficiency in Spanish vs. English were a function of age, migration history from Puerto Rico, sociopolitical identity, and social circumstances of speech. English appeared to replace Spanish as the dominant or preferred language among Puerto Ricans who were younger and born in the United States. Mature adults who were likely to have visited, lived in, or been schooled in Puerto Rico showed the highest rates of preference and ability to speak both Spanish and English. Older persons who were born in Puerto Rico and had the longest history of experiences there showed virtual monolingualism in Spanish.

As is the case with Mexican Americans, bilingual New York City Puerto Ricans often intermix use of Spanish and English when in conversation with peers. Poplack (1981) has found that there is a relatively stable set of rules for how language switches can occur within sentences, these rules being based on knowledge of morphological and syntactical rules of both Spanish and English. The general hypothesis emerging from studies of Spanish-English bilingualism among Puerto Ricans in New York City is that there exists a broad allegiance to maintenance of Spanish as a marker of cultural, social, and political identity, and at the same time a view that English is compatible with Puerto Rican culture in the context of the United States (Attinasi, 1979). Evidence also exists that some New York City Puerto Ricans (e.g., youth of lower socioeconomic background) adopt English and Spanish speech varieties that contrast noticeably with the so-called "standard varieties" of English and Spanish, these nonstandard variations being markers of social identity (Language Policy Task Force, 1980). Reyes (1981) and others have found evidence that borrowing of verb forms from English into Spanish often follows very similar syntactic rules, for both Puerto Ricans in New York and Chicanos in the Southwest. These observations suggest that Spanish-English contact in the United States may lead to regularities in how new Spanish word forms arise in a U.S. context.

In his comparative investigation of language variation among Hispanic subgroups, Laosa (1975) found that his New York City Puerto Rican children informants tended to follow the same language choice patterns in settings outside of school as the language choice patterns followed at home by parents. However, Puerto Rican children were found to use more English at school than at home, in cases where their parents spoke an intermixture of Spanish and English at home.

Possibly the first demographic study of language background factors affecting Puerto Rican New York students' access to college was done in 1953 by the New York City Board of Education. Known as the "Puerto Rican Study," this work advocated formulation of a uniform policy for assessment of non-English speaking students' language proficiency in English and subsequent assignment of students as needed to English-as-a-second-language classes (Santiago, 1978). The study in question was motivated by the failure of school district efforts to improve the low educational achievement of Puerto Rican students in public schools. While the study drew attention to the need for language assessment, it did not lead immediately to city-wide coordinated efforts for language placement and educational services for bilingual children. In 1974, the New York City Board of Education entered into a consent decree with Aspira as a result of a court suit brought by the latter that alleged unequal educational opportunity for students of limited English-speaking ability in New York schools.

At the state level in New York in 1970, an organization known as the Puerto Rican Education Association produced a report, *The Education of the Puerto Rican Child in New York,* for a state commission on educational finance (Santiago, 1978). The report recommended that English-as-a-second-language training for non-English speaking students was not to be favored, in terms of cost or outcome, over a bilingual curriculum. A bilingual curriculum was judged to be a more effective program to enhance educational progress among students who had substantial fluency in a non-English language (Santiago, 1978).

A recent major survey study of Puerto Rican high school students' achievement by Alicea and Mathis (1975) found that Puerto Rican students' ability to remain in high school and achieve graduation was very much related to students' judgments of their command of English. Dropouts were more likely to report that Spanish was their first language and that they possessed greater speaking, reading, and writing skills in Spanish than in English. Over one-quarter of high school dropouts reported both Spanish and English as their native languages. However, these same students tended to report lower levels of proficiency overall in both languages in comparison to other Puerto Rican students who remained in high school. Alicea and Mathis (1975) also found that Puerto Rican students from Spanish language backgrounds who remained in high school tended to have parents who were literate as opposed to nonliterate in Spanish.

While language proficiency factors are clearly important in Puerto Rican students' educational attainment, a number of other background factors have been found to interact along with language in affecting school success. The Alicea and Mathis (1975) study identified additional factors leading to persistence in high school, such as communication with parents, parental guidance and support in education, presence of significant adults at school providing help and encouragement, knowledge of and pride in Puerto Rican cultural heritage, students' perceptions of broader societal opportunities, and students' professional and higher education goals.

Attention is now turned to selected research findings on Cuban Americans' language characteristics, background, and educational attainment.

The most distinguishing demographic characteristics of the U.S. Cuban American Hispanic population is its relatively recent origin in the United States in significant numbers. About 80 percent of Cuban Americans residing in the United States in 1976 were born outside the United States, mostly in Cuba (U.S. Department of Health, Education, and Welfare, NCES, 1978b). Portes, McLeod, and Parker (1978) point out that the socioeconomic and familial education background of Cuban refugees tended to be stratified into two segments as of 1978. More recent immigration of Cubans into the United States since 1978 complexifies the characteristics of the present U.S. Cuban American population.

Cuban refugees arriving in the United States just after the Cuban Revolution in 1959 were more likely to represent the higher socioeconomic and educational backgrounds of Cuban society, while later refugees (after 1973) reflected lower socioeconomic status and educational backgrounds (Portes, et al., 1978). For example, median education in years for Cuban-born U.S. residents in 1969 was 11.3 years, in contrast to 8.6 years for Cuban immigrants in the period 1973–74 (Portes, et al., 1978).

Results of a sociological study of factors underlying aspirations of a sample of 590 Cuban refugees in the fall of 1973 and spring of 1974 by Portes, et al. (1978) showed that, for this group of later refugees, high self-judgments of knowledge of English was a major factor contributing to the prediction of higher educational aspiration among respondents. In contrast, high self-judgments of English proficiency did not significantly predict either occupational or income aspirations of refugees. However, past educational attainment was found to significantly predict educational, occupational, and income aspirations of refugees (Portes, et al., 1978). The same investigation further contrasted factors underlying aspirations of a sample of 822 Mexican immigrants to the United States at the Laredo and El Paso, Texas, ports of entry with the data from Cuban refugees. The analysis of the resulting Mexican immigrant data indicated that self-judged knowledge of English was a significant factor in predicting educational, occupational, and income aspirations. Past education was not as important a predictor of aspirations for Mexican immigrants as for Cuban refugees; Mexican immigrants showed an average of only 5.8 years of education prior to 1973–74 immigration to the United States (Portes, et al., 1978, p. 251).

The comparative research of Laosa (1975), mentioned earlier, also analyzed language use patterns of a sample of Cuban Americans in Miami. Laosa found that Cuban American parents who used English as the most frequent home language tended to have children who preferred to use English at home. Unlike Puerto Rican children, and more like Mexican American children, Cuban American children were likely to use much less Spanish than adult family members, even in home contexts. The Cuban American patterns of language use reported by Laosa suggested that children relied on Spanish when other children or adults also used Spanish in a setting, with a consistent trend of more use of English among children than among parents.

The Cuban American refugee reactions to the educational needs of children led to the rediscovery and modern development of bilingual education in the United States. In the early 1960s following mass immigration to the United States, Cuban refugees were able to gain sponsorship of bilingual education programs for children in Dade County, Florida, at the Coral Way School in Miami (Ogletree, 1978). The success of these programs came to act as a general stimulant to other Hispanics' concern for the development of bilingual programs throughout the nation.

CONCLUSIONS AND DISCUSSION

Appreciation of factors underlying Hispanics' opportunities to achieve in college rests on an ability to understand the characteristics of the U.S. Hispanic population as they may affect or be associated with opportunity to learn. The material reviewed in this chapter clearly establishes that the U.S. Hispanic population differs from the U.S. population at large. The evidence cited indicates that Hispanics' educational access and ability to complete schooling successfully are related to a number of background and demographic factors. If we wish to understand how and why Hispanics perform in college as they do, we need to develop sensitivity to the range of students' experiences that has accompanied an opportunity to attend college.

The demographic and educational survey data reviewed in this chapter lead to the conclusion that, by and large, Hispanics do not partake of the same educational opportunities as the U.S. nonminority population. In the data reviewed, there was incontrovertible evidence that Hispanics are less likely than other students to finish high school and become candidates for college admission. Beyond high school, the data reviewed show that Hispanics are less likely than majority group members to successfully complete college, receive degrees, and pursue advanced college training. A further interesting fact is that Hispanics enrolled in college tend to concentrate in two-year rather than four-year institutions. There is also the strong possibility that Hispanics tend to congregate in relatively low-prestige college institutions.

Lack of educational attainment among Hispanics is associated with income level of students' families, well-being of families and familial obligations, and language background of students. The foregoing factors are associated with Hispanic educational attainment at levels that are greater than those for white non-Hispanics. The present chapter has not addressed other factors that contribute to Hispanics' low level of educational attainment as these factors affect the opportunity to attend college. Among the most important remaining factors are students' academic achievement, motivation for college work, the quality of classroom instruction, sociocultural values of students, and the resources of institutions to meet the needs of students. Three of these further factors — academic achievement, quality of classroom instruction, and sociocultural values — are overviewed in the next chapter. The last chapter of the report also adds concern for institutional factors.

The U.S. Hispanic populace is heterogeneous in terms of its Latin American origin, history of immigration to the United States and settlement and migration in the United States, population size, age, income, language background, and educational attainment. While Hispanics overall are less likely to attain and complete college, an understanding of the factors associated with educational attainment should be coupled with a close look at major patterns of diversity among Hispanic students. Study of the demographic and background characteristics of the largest U.S. Hispanic subgroups — Cuban Americans, Mexican Americans, and Puerto Ricans — shows that there are both similarities and differences across subpopulations that are associated with level of educational attainment of each group. Furthermore, within each subpopulation there is substantial diversity in demographic and background characteristics of subgroup members that are associated with educational attainment.

For all groups, economic level of families and strength of English language background is associated with level of educational attainment. As a whole, Cuban Americans demonstrate a higher income level than either Mexican Americans or Puerto Ricans; they also demonstrate greater rates of access to college than the other two groups. While all three Hispanic subgroups show strong exposure to the Spanish language, Cubans show more exposure to and use of Spanish than Puerto Ricans or Mexican Americans, in that order. A Spanish-language background is not necessarily associated with lack of an English-language background. Survey data on language background and sociolinguistic research reveal that Hispanics vary in their frequency of using both Spanish and English and in the social circumstances in which they rely on each language. Across generations, starting with U.S. Hispanic students born outside the United States and going on to generations of children of Hispanic parents born in the United States, there appears to be an increase in Hispanics' reliance on English across succeeding generations along with a decline in the use of Spanish. At present, not enough is known about demographic factors that might produce an increase in Hispanics' use of Spanish, though this possibility exists due to increased concentrations of Hispanics in some regions of the country.

Across all Hispanic subgroups, Hispanics attaining college show a strong background exposure to Spanish. Interestingly, Cuban Americans show the most background exposure to Spanish and also the highest frequency of college attendance among Hispanics.

Sociolinguistic research on the Spanish-language and English-language practices of Hispanic subgroups indicates that Hispanic subgroups show familiarity with a number of varieties of Spanish other than a variety that might be termed "standard." Varieties of spoken Spanish are associated with Hispanic subgroup identity, geographical area of residence, and social affiliations of speakers. Educational history of a family and exposure to standard Spanish in schooling may lead to substantial variance in functional knowledge of Spanish. Families' literacy background in Spanish may be an important factor surrounding children's learning of Spanish and ways in which bilingual education may facilitate children's learning.

The spoken and written English of Hispanics can show effects stemming from knowledge of Spanish, and this may be a factor in educational performance in English. Oral or reading comprehension in English also may show effects of knowledge of Spanish, though this latter point was not pursued in the chapter. At the level of word-sound (phonology), word-formation (morphology), spelling (orthography), and syntax, there exist well-known phenomena that demonstrate transfer of elements of Spanish into English. Sociolinguistic research has established that some of these forms of transfer come to be socially acceptable and even expected in the English communication of Hispanics in some social networks. However, it is still the case that such transfer is likely to be regarded as dysfunctional in English school settings and in English academic tasks. Some research on Hispanics' English essay writing reveals that lack of higher-level skills in organization of the structure of essays and lack of logical clarity in statements characterize Hispanics' poorer essay performance. It is alleged that these sorts of infelicities reflect poor literacy training in school more than transfer of Spanish language characteristics into English writing. Further discussion of the specific impact of language skills on Hispanics' education experience prior to college, college admissions profile, and college performance is given in subsequent chapters.

The next chapter focuses on research findings describing Hispanics' preparation for college, as revealed by surveys of high school achievement and data on factors affecting high school achievement.

Achievement of Hispanic
High School Students

In order to understand the characteristics of Hispanics who become candidates for college, it is valuable to consider first the characteristics of the larger national pool of Hispanic high school students
from which Hispanic college students emerge. To be sure, the population of Hispanic high school students who eventually become college
candidates for admission is different from Hispanic high school students at large, but some of the ways in which the two populations differ
are not always clear. As evidence indicates, it is plausible that some of
the factors that constrain Hispanics' level of achievement in high
school may also constrain Hispanics' achievement in college. This
chapter begins with a review of selective findings from major national
survey studies that included data on Hispanics' high school achievement. Subsequently, attention is turned to further findings of research
studies that add to an understanding of how language background,
socioeconomic characteristics, schooling characteristics, cultural background, and socialization are associated with Hispanics' high school
and general schooling achievement. Issues that address the importance of school resources or school finance on quality of schooling are
not discussed in depth in this chapter, though they undoubtedly are significant contributors to the school learning opportunities of Hispanics
(e.g., see Olivas, 1981, and Carter and Segura, 1979, for a review of
these concerns).

RECENT NATIONAL DATA ON HISPANICS'
HIGH SCHOOL ACHIEVEMENT

Discussion of achievement level of Hispanic high school students
starts with a comparison of Hispanic versus white non-Hispanic seniors' grades. Data from the National Longitudinal Study of the High
School Class of 1972 (*CEH, 1980*, pp. 68–69) given in Table 7 reveal
that Hispanic high school seniors generally received lower grades than

Table 7

The Percent Distribution of Grades of Hispanic and White High School Seniors: 1972

Grade[1]	Hispanic	White, non-Hispanic
Total	100.0	100.0
Mostly A (90–100)	3.7	10.4
About half A, half B (85–89)	15.5	20.7
Mostly B (80–89)	15.7	21.3
About half B, half C (75–79)	35.6	26.8
Mostly C (70–74)	17.6	13.8
About half C, half D (65–69)	10.8	5.9
Mostly D (60–64)	0.5	0.9
Mostly below D (below 60)	0.6	0.1

[1] Numerical average is in parentheses.
NOTE: Details may not add to totals because of rounding.

SOURCE: U.S. Department of Health, Education, and Welfare, National Center for Education Statistics, *National Longitudinal Study of the High School Class of 1972, Student Questionnaire and Test Results by Sex, High School Program, Ethnic Category, and Father's Education,* 1975, as cited in U.S. Department of Education, National Center for Education Statistics, *The Condition of Education for Hispanic Americans.* Compiled and edited by G. H. Brown, N. Rosen, and M. A. Olivas. Washington, D.C.: 1980, p. 68.

their white non-Hispanic classmates. In the grade-point intervals of "mostly B grades or better" and above, only 34.9 percent of Hispanic students were represented as opposed to 52.4 percent of white non-Hispanic students. To the extent that this result is representative of the general population of high school Hispanics and white non-Hispanics during 1972, it indicates a clear deficit in Hispanics' achievement relative to whites' achievement, without regard for information about curriculum choices of students and college aspirations of students.

Some indication of grade-point average differences among Hispanic and white non-Hispanic high school students ostensibly planning college attendance is found by study of grade-point average distributions among students taking College Board Admissions Testing Program tests during 1979–80. Based on unpublished College Board data, Table 8 reveals, when aggregated, that 54.6 percent Mexican Americans, 46.3 percent Puerto Ricans, and 60.9 percent white non-His-

Table 8

Overall High School Grade Averages of Mexican Americans, Puerto Ricans, and Non-Hispanic Whites Taking College Board Admissions Testing Program Tests in 1979–80

Overall high school grade average[1]	Percent Mexican Americans	Percent Puerto Ricans	Percent white, non-Hispanics
3.75–4.00	12.1	7.4	16.9
3.50–3.74	11.5	8.6	12.9
3.25–3.49	12.8	11.5	13.5
3.00–3.24	18.2	18.8	17.6
2.75–2.99	12.9	13.8	12.0
2.50–2.74	13.0	15.2	11.6
2.25–2.49	9.3	10.4	7.2
2.00–2.24	6.6	9.0	5.1
Under 2.00	3.6	5.4	3.1
Mean GPA	3.01	2.88	3.10
Number responding	15,239	7,258	739,421

[1] Self-report grade-point average based on course work in the six subject areas of English, mathematics, foreign languages, biological sciences, physical sciences, and social studies.

panics judged they had grade-point averages 3.0 (letter grade B) or above. These results show that Hispanic College Board examinees in 1979–80 manifested noticeably lower high school grades than white non-Hispanics. Care should be taken not to infer that the students reported in Table 8 necessarily went on to apply formally to colleges. Also, it should be noted that Hispanic examinees taking College Board Admissions Testing Program tests are not likely to be representative of the full population of Hispanics planning college attendance in any given year, since large numbers of Hispanic college candidates seek enrollment in two-year colleges that are less likely to require college admissions test scores from applicants.

Attention is now turned to data regarding Hispanics' learning achievement in high school based on use of testing instruments. Table 9 presents achievement test scores of Hispanic and white non-Hispanic high school students in five learning areas in the period 1971–1975,

Table 9

Achievement in Five Subject Matter Areas for Hispanic and White Students, 9-, 13-, and 17-year-olds: 1971–75

Subject matter and ethnic group	Percentage point difference[1] from the national average for:		
	9-year-olds	13-year-olds	17-year-olds
Social studies			
Hispanic	−10.59	−10.05	−13.12
White, non-Hispanic	2.73	2.07	2.39
Science			
Hispanic	−9.53	−11.55	−11.08
White, non-Hispanic	3.12	3.49	2.13
Mathematics			
Hispanic	−7.77	−11.71	−14.36
White, non-Hispanic	2.76	3.74	3.63
Career and occupational development			
Hispanic	−14.08	−12.44	−7.65
White, non-Hispanic	3.23	3.50	2.19
Reading			
Hispanic	−10.77	−11.25	−11.42
White, non-Hispanic	2.54	2.73	2.78

[1] All of the differences from the national norm in this table are statistically significant at the 0.05 level.

SOURCE: U.S. Department of Health, Education, and Welfare, National Center for Education Statistics, National Assessment of Education Progress, *Hispanic Student Achievement in Five Learning Areas: 1971–75,* as cited in U.S. Department of Education, National Center for Education Statistics, *The Condition of Education for Hispanic Americans.* Compiled and edited by G. H. Brown, N. Rosen, and M. A. Olivas. Washington, D.C.: 1980, p. 222.

Figure 5

Achievement in Five Subject Matter Areas

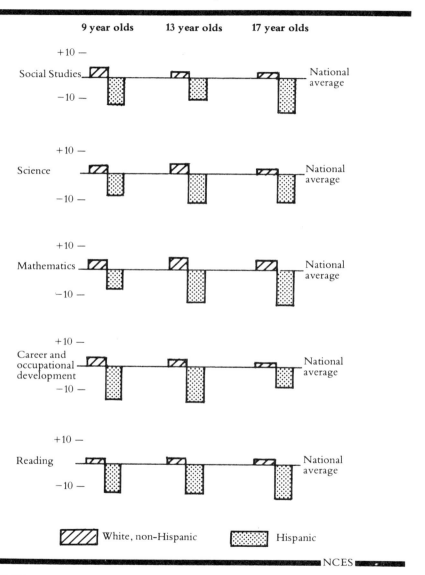

| | 9 year olds | 13 year olds | 17 year olds |

SOURCE: U.S. Department of Education, National Center for Education Statistics, *The Condition of Education for Hispanic Americans*. Compiled and edited by G. H. Brown, N. Rosen, and M. A. Olivas. Washington, D.C.: 1980, p. 223.

based on the National Assessment of Education Progress (*CEH, 1980,* p. 222).[4] Figure 5 (*CEH, 1980,* p. 223) presents the same data in graphic format. The entries in Table 9 indicate the difference in percentage of test items answered correctly in a given achievement area by Hispanics and white non-Hispanics relative to the average percent of items answered correctly in the same achievement area by students nationally. As indicated by Table 9 and Figure 5, Hispanic high school students aged nine, thirteen, and seventeen years scored lower at a statistically significant level than white non-Hispanic students of the same age in each of the five learning achievement areas: social studies, science, mathematics, career and educational development, and reading.

Just recently, 1980 data from the High School and Beyond longitudinal study of high school sophomores and seniors have become available (Nielsen and Fernandez, 1981). The study is noteworthy for this report because it involved a sample of 6,698 Hispanic high school students who were oversampled randomly from the population of high school students at large. The strategy of oversampling permitted adequate numbers of Hispanics from each of several Hispanic subgroups to be included in order to support data analyses on achievement broken down by Hispanic subgroup membership. The schooling variables included measures of school delay, schooling aspirations, and cognitive achievement. The High School and Beyond study of 1980 also involved administration of an elaborate questionnaire that elicited information from respondents on: a) family background (father's education and family income); b) immigration history (nativity, length of U.S. residence of students, and length of U.S. residence of mother); and c) language characteristics (home language, mother tongue, Spanish proficiency, English proficiency, and Spanish use).

In this report, we will restrict discussion of Hispanics' achievement on the 1980 High School and Beyond study to achievement test scores in the three areas of mathematics, reading, and vocabulary.[5] Table 10 displays achievement test score data for high school sophomores and seniors in the spring 1980 broken down by the following ethnic/racial classifications: Mexican American, Cuban, Puerto Rican; other Latin American; black non-Hispanic; and white non-Hispanic. Inspection of the average achievement scores in the areas of mathematics, reading, and vocabulary for both high school sophomores and seniors shows that all Hispanic subgroups performed uniformly lower than white non-Hispanics in every cognitive achievement area that was assessed. Overall, white non-Hispanics tended to show about a one standard deviation advantage over Hispanics on all achievement tests. Among Hispanics,

Table 10

Cognitive Achievement Scores on Mathematics, Reading, and Vocabulary Tests by Population Subgroup: Spring 1980

Subgroup	Mathematics			Reading			Vocabulary		
	Sample size	Mean score	Standard deviation	Sample size	Mean score	Standard deviation	Sample size	Mean score	Standard deviation
Sophomores									
Mexican American	1,864	7.5	3.5	1,865	2.7	1.7	1,862	2.9	1.6
Cuban	259	8.7	4.3	248	3.5	2.1	254	3.4	2.1
Puerto Rican	313	7.1	3.2	311	2.7	1.8	316	3.0	1.6
Other Latin American	659	8.0	3.4	660	3.0	1.8	659	3.2	1.8
Non-Hispanic black	868	6.7	3.2	873	2.5	1.7	872	2.7	1.6
Non-Hispanic white	930	10.3	3.8	931	3.9	2.0	933	4.1	1.9
Seniors									
Mexican American	1,621	8.4	4.0	1,632	3.3	1.9	1,628	3.5	1.8
Cuban	286	10.1	4.3	292	3.9	2.1	292	4.2	1.9
Puerto Rican	257	8.0	4.6	262	3.3	2.0	265	3.5	1.9
Other Latin American	557	8.3	3.9	565	3.3	1.9	567	3.6	1.9
Non-Hispanic black	854	7.7	3.8	854	3.2	2.0	856	3.2	1.8
Non-Hispanic white	893	11.6	4.0	901	4.9	2.0	898	4.8	1.9

NOTE: Means and standard deviation are weighted.

SOURCE: Nielsen, F., and Fernandez, R. M. *High School and Beyond Study: Achievement of Hispanic Students in U.S. Schools.* Chicago: National Opinion Research Center (in preparation).

Cuban-origin students showed the highest performance levels in all achievement areas, but these performance levels consistently were below those of white non-Hispanic students. The achievement levels of Mexican Americans and Puerto Ricans differed indistinguishably from each other and were uniformly lower than Cuban student achievement levels in all areas. Care should be taken in interpreting the achievement differences demonstrated by these data. The reported results can be used to generalize only about the portions of the Hispanic populace in 1980 that were actually enrolled in high school and were represented by the sample of Hispanics generated. Specifically excluded, for example, are Hispanic students of high school age who dropped out of school before sophomore or senior standing in spring 1980.

Preliminary analyses of the Hispanic High School and Beyond 1980 study have indicated that aggregate Hispanic subgroup achievement test scores for sophomores and seniors in each of the three areas of mathematics, reading, and vocabulary were significantly predictable in regression analyses from predictor measures of Spanish- and English-language characteristics, length of U.S. residence, socioeconomic status, gender, and in some instances Hispanic subgroup membership (Nielsen and Fernandez, 1981). While still subject to further interpretation and clarification, the preliminary results of analyses indicate that self-judgments of overall proficiency level in either Spanish or English acted as positive predictors of high school achievement, though the predictive relationship was stronger based on self-judgments of proficiency in English than on self-judgments of proficiency in Spanish. Self-judgments of proficiency in each language were determined by adding up Likert scale judgments of proficiency in each of the four modalities: oral comprehension, speaking, reading, and writing.

A composite variable, "Spanish-use," representing judged frequency of oral interaction in Spanish between students and parents was found to be a significant negative predictor of achievement in all subject areas for both sophomore and senior high school grade levels. In contrast, as mentioned, regression analyses revealed that judged Spanish proficiency served as a positive predictor of achievement. These findings suggest that, somehow, more frequent oral use of Spanish at home was allied with poorer achievement test performance, while overall verbal ability in Spanish contributed positively to achievement test performance in English. For a fuller understanding of these results, it would need to be determined what other sorts of variables are confounded with the two types of language measures described and also with academic achievement.

Other results of the regression analyses for predicting sophomore and senior Hispanics' scholastic achievement showed that Puerto Ricans and Mexican Americans did not differ from each other in their achievement levels in reading and vocabulary for both sophomore and senior high school years, once the effect of other language and background variables was taken into account. Mathematics achievement scores of Puerto Rican senior high school students did not differ significantly from the corresponding scores of Mexican American senior high school students, after the influence of other language and background variables on achievement was accounted for. In the case of sophomores, however, Mexican Americans significantly outperformed Puerto Ricans in mathematics even with control for influences of language and background factors on school achievement. Cuban sophomores and seniors significantly outperformed Mexican Americans in all achievement test areas, after control for the influence of language and background factors on academic achievement.

Factors Affecting Hispanics' High School Achievement

While segments of the High School and Beyond data of 1980 thus far analyzed (Nielsen and Fernandez, 1981) investigated how high school achievement test scores of Hispanics were associated with ethnic subgroup membership and background factors, other research data not involving test scores exist that relate the quality of Hispanics' high school experiences and achievement to background factors. The review of studies that follows is not intended to be a complete one by any means. Rather, it should serve to alert the reader to factors that potentially affect Hispanics' achievement in high school and possibly in college as well. The discussion starts with a consideration of high school seniors' perceptions of the problems underlying their ability to learn in school. Afterwards, the discussion reviews a study of sociological factors affecting recidivism in high school. Finally, research is examined that investigates how communication and sociocultural factors may affect Hispanics' interaction in classroom settings and their achievement test performance.

Table 11 and Figure 6 (*CEH, 1980*, pp. 70–71) present data from the National Longitudinal Study of the High School Class of 1972 that display Hispanic and white non-Hispanic senior high school students' judgments of factors that were important sources of interference with school work. Inspection of Table 11 and Figure 6 reveals that both Hispanic and white non-Hispanic senior high school students agreed more or less to the same extent that the following factors inhibited school work: "School doesn't offer courses I want to take"; "I don't feel part of the school"; "Poor teaching"; "Poor study habits"; "I find it hard to adjust to the school routine"; "My job takes too much time." The following set of factors obstructing school work were cited between 5 and 10 percent more frequently by Hispanic seniors than by white non-Hispanic seniors: "Courses are too hard"; "Teachers don't help me enough"; "My own ill health"; "Transportation to school is difficult." The greatest discrepancy between Hispanic and white non-Hispanic seniors in judgment of factors obstructing school work occurred for reasons that had to do with the characteristics of the familial life of students and the compatibility of home life with school learning activities. Each of the following factors obstructing school work was cited by more than one-third of Hispanic seniors at a level at least 10 percent higher than for white non-Hispanics: "Worry over money problems (repayment of loan, support of dependents, family income, etc.)"; "Family obligations (other than money problems)"; "Lack of good place to study at home"; "Parents aren't interested in my education."

Investigations of background factors affecting Hispanics' high school attainment or achievement by and large are not of a survey character. Discussion of one important exception to this pattern follows.

Investigation of reasons underlying Puerto Rican students' high dropout rate prior to high school graduation was the subject of a survey study in seven major urban areas by Aspira of America (1976). Based on 1970 Census data, this survey reported that 60 percent of Puerto Rican youths dropped out of school prior to high school graduation. Among those graduating, 25 percent were delayed by more than one year. Aspira concluded that the delay/dropout pattern observed could be explained in large part by low parental level of schooling, low socioeconomic status of parents, low financial support of schools, and low population density of a Spanish-origin community in which students lived. In addition to the direct effect of these factors on delayed schooling, a separate index labeled "community poverty and degree of recent migration" was found to directly and strongly affect delay/dropout rates of Puerto Ricans. This factor also indirectly affected delay/dropout rates because it was correlated with the other explanatory variables mentioned.

In the Aspira study, students who encountered difficulty in matriculating to the next grade by the ages of thirteen to fifteen showed the highest dropout rate from high school by the ages of sixteen to eighteen. Strong differences in dropout rates were found according to geographical/urban area of residence. Puerto Ricans in the West Coast cities of Los Angeles and San Francisco were less likely to drop out of high school than students in major East Coast and Midwest urban areas.

Table 11

Factors Cited by Hispanic and White High School Seniors as Interfering with Their School Work: 1972

Factors	Percentage[1] who answered "somewhat" or "a great deal"	
	Hispanic	White, non-Hispanic
Worry over money problems (repayment of loan, support of dependents, family income, etc.)	45.5	27.4
Family obligations (other than money problems)	39.3	23.6
Lack of a good place to study at home	36.7	22.1
Parents aren't interested in my education	33.7	19.4
Courses are too hard	49.9	41.0
Teachers don't help me enough	54.1	47.3
My own ill health	16.7	10.3
Transportation to school is difficult	15.9	9.6
School doesn't offer the courses I want to take	45.5	50.3
Don't feel part of the school	39.5	35.5
Poor teaching	46.4	50.3
Poor study habits	59.7	57.2
Find it hard to adjust to school routine	24.3	22.9
My job takes too much time	19.1	19.3

[1] Students could make multiple responses. Factors are listed in descending order of the size of difference between Hispanics and white, non-Hispanics.

SOURCE: U.S. Department of Health, Education, and Welfare, National Center for Education Statistics, *National Longitudinal Study of the High School Class of 1972, Student Questionnaire and Test Results by Sex, High School Program, Ethnic Category and Father's Education,* 1975. As cited in U.S. Department of Education, National Center for Education Statistics, *The Condition of Education for Hispanic Americans.* Compiled and edited by G. H. Brown, N. Rosen, and M. A. Olivas. Washington, D.C.: 1980, p. 70.

Figure 6

Factors Interfering with School Work of High School Seniors

Relatively more His-
panic than white high
school seniors cited
family-related factors
as interfering with their
school work.

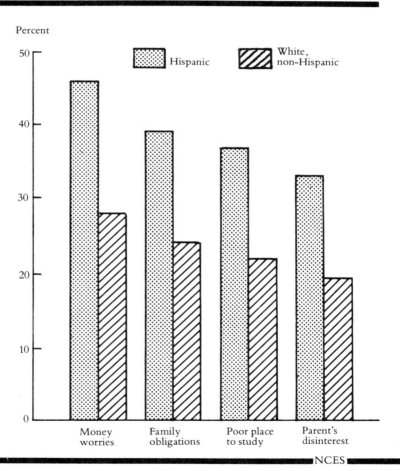

SOURCE: U.S. Department of Education, National Center for Education Statistics, *The Condition of Education for Hispanic Americans.* Compiled and edited by G. H. Brown, N. Rosen, and
M. A. Olivas. Washington, D.C.: 1980, p. 71.

This disparity in dropout rates was explained in interpretation of data analysis by the higher socioeconomic and educational status among Puerto Rican families in the West versus elsewhere.

Attention will now be given to a study of factors influencing Mexican Americans' opportunities to learn in classrooms. In a major study of Mexican American education at the fourth, eighth, tenth, and twelfth grades, The U.S. Commission on Civil Rights (1973) found that teacher-student communication patterns were distinctly different for Chicano versus Anglo students. Figures 7, 8, and 9 taken from the report, *Teachers and Students Report V: Differences in Teacher Interaction with Mexican American and Anglo Students* (pp. 27, 29, 31), display some major differences in teachers' interaction patterns with Mexican American versus Anglo students. Teachers were found to direct praise or encouragement to Anglo students 36 percent more often than to Mexican American students. Teachers used or built on the spoken contributions of Anglo students 40 percent more often than they did for Mexican American students; they also asked Anglo students 20 percent more questions in class than they asked Mexican Americans. These results suggest that the qualitative character of communicative participation and opportunity to learn in classroom settings was distinctly inferior for Mexican American students. The results further raise the possibility that language proficiency in English per se among Mexican American students might not be solely responsible for quality of communication in classrooms.

The results discussed suggest that teachers' negative attitudes toward and low expectations of Mexican American students also may contribute to low quality of classroom experiences for Mexican Americans. Interestingly, Figure 7 suggests that the 36 Mexican American teachers described praised Anglo students at a higher rate than Anglo teachers did. Figure 7 also shows that Mexican American teachers did not praise Mexican American children at a higher rate than Anglo teachers did. The Mexican American teacher data may not be reliable or representative since so few Mexican American teachers were studied.

In discussing his own research on kindergarten and early-school-grade Mexican American children's interaction with teachers, Laosa (1977b) suggested that the findings in the U.S. Commission on Civil Rights report on student-teacher interactions failed to fully investigate how students' language dominance in English might have affected the conclusions drawn in that same report. On the basis of his own research, Laosa (1977b, p. 61) concluded that "students' language dominance — rather than student ethnic group membership — was the significant factor influencing teachers' disapproving behavior toward students."

Figure 7

Average Amount of Per-Pupil Praise or Encouragement Given to Individual Mexican American and Anglo Students by Mexican American and Anglo Teachers

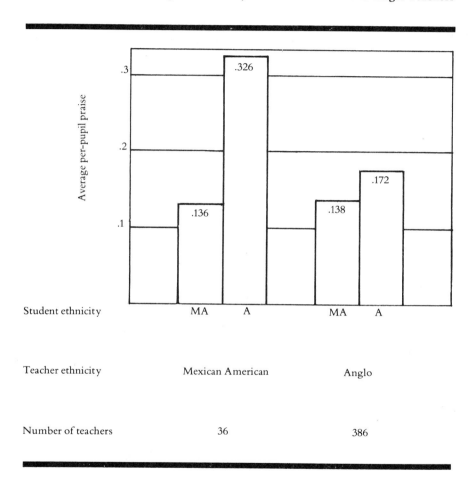

| Student ethnicity | MA | A | MA | A |

| Teacher ethnicity | Mexican American | Anglo |

| Number of teachers | 36 | 386 |

SOURCE: U.S. Commission on Civil Rights, *Mexican American Education Study, Report 5: Teachers and Students*, Washington, D.C.: 1973, p. 27.

Figure 8

**Average Amount of Acceptance and Use of Student Ideas Per Pupil Given by
Teachers to Individual Mexican American and Anglo Students**

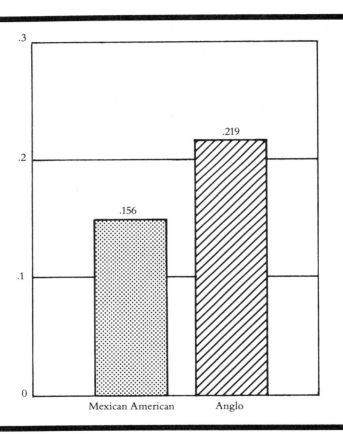

SOURCE: U.S. Commission on Civil Rights, *Mexican American Education Study, Report 5:
Teachers and Students*. Washington, D.C.: 1973, p. 29.

Figure 9

Average Amount of Acceptance and Use of Student Ideas Per Pupil Given to
Individual Mexican and Anglo Students by Teachers in Schools with Various
Degrees of Ethnic Concentration

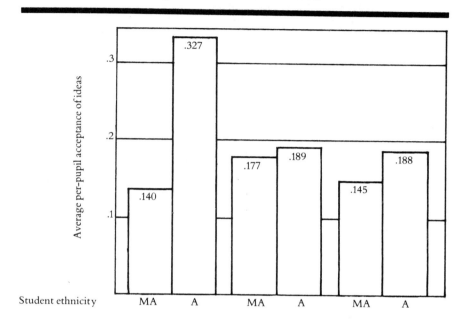

Student ethnicity MA A	MA A	MA A
Degree of ethnic concentration within the school* Low	Medium	High
Number of classrooms 96	163	174

*The degree of ethnic concentration within the school represents the extent to which there is variation in the ethnic composition of classrooms within a school. In low ethnic concentration schools, Mexican American students appear to be distributed evenly among the classrooms. In medium ethnic concentration schools, there is a tendency for Mexican Americans to be found in some classrooms more than others. In high ethnic concentration schools, Mexican Americans are definitely isolated in specific classrooms.

SOURCE: U.S. Commission on Civil Rights, *Mexican American Education Study, Report 5: Teachers and Students,* Washington, D.C.: 1973, p. 31.

Again, to quote Laosa on his own findings (p. 60):

> For both the Anglo American and the Mexican American
> students whose dominant language was English there was
> a decrement from kindergarten to second-grade classrooms
> in the frequency of disapprovals received from teachers.
> For the non-English dominant Mexican American stu-
> dents there was an increase from kindergarten to second-
> grade classrooms in the number of disapprovals received
> from teachers. The results applied equally to male and
> female students.

The proficiency issue raised by Laosa (1977b) in accounting for
some of the occurrences of negative interactions between Mexican
American students and teachers appears to be supported by the findings
of research on teachers' attitudes toward language variation among high-
school-age Hispanics. In a thorough review of experimental research
on teachers' attitudes toward Mexican American students' speech,
Ramirez (1981) cited persistent evidence that both Anglo and Hispanic teachers were prone to attribute negative qualities toward students who demonstrated accented English, use of a nonstandard variety
of English, or use of nonstandard Spanish. Negative attributions re-
currently denigrated students' academic capabilities and potential to
achieve in school on the basis of students' nonstandard speech patterns. The research of Ryan and Carranza (1975) on Mexican American, black, and Anglo attitudes towards Mexican American high school
students' accented English found that, in general, speakers of accented
English were judged to have less social status than speakers of standard
English. Judgments of low status included attributions of low educational attainment and low intelligence. Thus, there is recurrent research evidence that negative attitudes towards Hispanics' nonstandard
or accented speech may impact negatively on Hispanics' school experiences.

Research on young, early-school-age Hispanic children's communicative competence (Carrasco, Vera, and Cazden, 1981; and Carrasco,
1981) suggests that language proficiency, viewed narrowly in terms of
pronunciation skills and knowledge of the surface rules of Spanish or
English, is not adequate in and of itself in accounting for children's
success or failure in classroom communication. The results of communicative competence research indicate that social and cultural factors
defining a communicative situation as a speech event, the set of social
roles played among interlocutors, and the sociolinguistic repertoire of
participants affect the success of communication in a classroom as
much, if not more than, surface proficiency in a language. To date, no

studies of young adult Hispanics' communicative competence in high school or college settings appear to exist.[6] Such studies would be valuable in understanding how the process of classroom communication affects students' participation and learning in classrooms at nonelementary levels. The research that has been mentioned here suggests that limited language proficiency in English, negative attitudes towards accented English or English showing influence of Spanish, and failure to adhere to expected sociocultural norms of communication can all jointly inhibit Hispanics' opportunities to learn and communicate in school settings.

Sociocultural and Socialization Factors Associated with Hispanics' Education

No insightful discussion of factors affecting Hispanics' educational opportunities would be complete without consideration of the impact of cultural background and socialization on Hispanics' educational achievement. In the course of the present review, no national survey studies of the impact of cultural factors and socialization on school achievement were encountered. The discussion that follows is built on existing summaries of research on cultural values and socialization factors found to affect young Hispanic children's schooling achievement. The commentary in this section is intended to be rudimentary, merely highlighting issues that for the most part are not investigated in social science research and educational research on high school age Hispanics.

In their volume *Mexican Americans in School: A Decade of Change,* Carter and Segura (1979) overviewed widely held cultural stereotypes that contrast the sociocultural values of Mexican Americans versus those of Anglos. While the Carter and Segura volume addressed only one major U.S. Hispanic subgroup, Mexican Americans, the span of concerns seems relevant in its broadest sense to the cultural conflicts and prejudices faced by other Hispanic subgroups in adjusting to the U.S. educational system.

Carter and Segura indicated that there exist many stereotypical folk notions of the value systems of Mexican Americans and Anglos, along with notions of how these value systems conflict. Examples of conflicting folk stereotypes of Mexican American and Anglo values are given in Table 12, based on previous analyses by Brischetto and Arciniega (1973) and Zintz (1963).

According to Carter and Segura, each pair of Mexican American and Anglo values listed in Table 12 implicitly conveys a negative attribution about how well Mexican Americans are predisposed to per-

Table 12

Classification of Major Differences Between Mexican American and Anglo American Value Systems

Mexican American Values	Anglo American Values
Children from traditional Spanish-speaking families may be said to have accepted these general patterns:	American school teachers are sure to place great value on these practices:
Subjugation to nature	Mastery over nature
Present time orientation	Future time orientation
Status based on ascription	Status based on achievement
Particularistic perspective	Universalistic perspective
Emotional	Affectively neutral
Low level of aspiration	High level of aspiration
Work for present needs	Work for future success
Sharing	Saving
Nonadherence to time schedules	Adherence to time schedules
Reaction to change	Acceptance of change
Nonscientific explanation for natural phenomena	Scientific explanation for all behavior
Humility	Competition
Obedience to the will of God	Individuality and self-realization

SOURCE: Brischetto and Arciñiega, p. 36; adapted from Zintz, 1963, pp. 241–243, as cited in Carter, R., and Segura, R., *Mexican Americans in School: A Decade of Change.* New York: College Entrance Examination Board, 1979, p. 84.

form in American schools. Thus, for example, Mexican Americans' alleged "present time orientation" versus Anglos' alleged "future time orientation" can be taken to imply that Mexican Americans are less likely than Anglos to view their personal development in terms of long-range objectives. In turn, this difference in values can be taken to imply that Mexican Americans will be less likely than Anglos to view their performance in school in terms of its consequences for long-range personal development.

Carter and Segura reviewed research studies that refute or support the validity of some of the cultural stereotypes given in Table 12 for Mexican Americans. The results of such studies suggested that many stereotypes of the sort listed in Table 12 are not valid. Where data did support differences in Mexican American and Anglo values, there was no control in studies for the influence of differences in socioeconomic background of respondents; this fact leads to a questioning of the validity of results, since socioeconomic level and not cultural orientation alone could lead to the differences observed. Some of the research cited by Carter and Segura showed no difference between Mexican Americans' and Anglos' cultural values. Carter and Segura concluded that the most important educational impact of cultural stereotypes, such as those listed in Table 12, is that they may be believed by teachers regardless of whether they are true or not. Teachers' belief in stereotypes contrasting the cultural values of Mexican Americans and Anglos may lead teachers to manifest negative expectations about the schooling potential and performance of Mexican Americans.

Discussion is now given to connections between cultural values and socialization practices that can affect Hispanic children's success in schooling in the long-range developmental span. Citing Ramirez and Castañeda's (1974, pp. 41–42) research on Mexican American children's socialization and cognitive style, Carter and Segura (1979, p. 115) identify major bona fide cultural value clusters of Mexican Americans as: "1) identification with family, community, and ethnic group; 2) personalization of interpersonal relationships; 3) status and role definition in family and community; 4) Mexican Catholic ideology." Each of these value clusters is theorized to be imparted to Mexican American children in their socialization, and to be propagated in individuals' development of cognitive styles. Cognitive styles are enduring ways in which persons come to perceive themselves and the world and enduring ways or styles of behaving. Categories of cognitive styles include, for example, learning styles, incentive-motivation styles, human-relational styles, and communication styles.[7]

In the context of the present review, it is impossible to survey the extensive research literature on Hispanic children's cognitive style. For a critical review of this research, the reader should refer to Kagan and Buriel's (1977) paper, "Field Dependence-Independence and Mexican American Culture and Education." The general thrust of the field dependence-independence research on Hispanic children has been that Hispanic children (tending to be more field dependent) prefer social cooperation and nonanalytic strategies of thought and problem solving in educational interactions. In contrast, Anglo children (tending to be more field independent) stress competition, independence, and more use of analytic modes of thought in school interactions. As a result of field dependence-independence research, some educators and researchers (e.g., see Ramirez and Castañeda, 1974) have contended that the educational system and teachers' styles of interaction should be manipulated to make education more accommodating to Mexican American children's cultural values and cognitive styles.

In a summary of some results from his extensive programmatic research on Hispanic children's socialization, Laosa (1982) has concluded that parents' educational attainment level is a preeminent and critical factor in children's development of cognitive styles related to cognitive schooling requirements. Educational attainment level of parents is a more important factor than Hispanic or Anglo ethnic identity in determining how parents — particularly mothers — teach their children to think. Hispanic mothers with more educational attainment are more likely to teach their children thinking skills by using praise in approval of correct behavior, and inquiry methods, whereby a mother directs a child's thought in problem solving through questions. In addition, Hispanic mothers with more educational attainment are less likely to use modeling (i.e., a mother showing a child how to actually solve a problem), and negative physical control (i.e., punishment of a child's inappropriate problem solving behavior). Laosa has also found that Hispanic parents with more educational attainment read from books more frequently to their children. In interpreting the findings of his program of research, Laosa suggests that Hispanic children's success or failure in the educational system is linked directly to children's socialization and learning of cognitive skills at home. At a more distal level, parents' educational attainment is the most critical factor in determining how parents socialize and prepare their children for schooling.

Attention is now briefly turned to another area of socialization that may impact on Hispanics' education. This area is racial integration of classrooms. At present, we do not have extensive evidence about how racial integration of classrooms affects Hispanics' school achievement. One well known study of desegregation by Gerard and Miller (1975) found that Mexican American children's school achievement was not affected negatively by school desegregation; this finding occurred in the southwest community of Riverside, California, with a relatively high population density of Mexican Americans. A major review of the impact of school desegregation on black children's school achievement by Crain and Mahard (1978) found substandard evidence that desegregation was often associated with achievement gains by black students. Working with 1972 National Longitudinal Survey data, Mahard (1978) found that high school academic achievement rates and attainment of college rates were higher for Puerto Ricans attending primarily Anglo schools. No such advantage was found for Mexican Americans, but Hispanic students in the category "other Latins" who lived in the West did show a significant positive effect on school achievement related to attending primarily Anglo schools. Thus, while the impact of classroom racial and social integration on Hispanic students' school achievement has not been investigated intensively, there is nationally based evidence that extent of classroom integration will be positively related to at least some Hispanics' school achievement.

CONCLUSIONS AND DISCUSSION

The research reviewed in this chapter has suggested that U.S. Hispanic high school students are deriving less academic preparation for college than white nonminority students. This evidence is based on the lower high school grades and lower achievement test scores of Hispanics relative to white nonminority students. Data was cited that demonstrated that Hispanic high school students manifested lower learning achievement in course areas critical to college preparation. Survey data discussed in Chapter 2 cited recidivism in school and dropping out of school as key factors affecting the educational attainment level of Hispanics.

Background and personal factors associated with Hispanics' lower levels of high school achievement were the same factors that underlay low level of educational attainment, recidivism, and dropping out of school, as outlined in reviews of national survey studies of Hispanics' educational attainment discussed in Chapter 2. Hispanic high school students' worries about their own well-being or their families' well-being were factors judged to affect high school performance negatively at a rate considerably higher than was the case for white non-Hispanic high school students. Lack of a home environment conducive to study and parents' lack of interest in children's educational goals were also cited more often as constraints to Hispanics' high school achievement than was the case for white non-Hispanics.

Language background of Hispanics showed a moderate-to-strong relationship to Hispanics' high school achievement, but the influence of language background on schooling may be mediated by other factors. Hispanic students' judgment of their degree of overall proficiency in English was positively related to their performance on high school achievement tests in English. Hispanic students' judgment of their overall *proficiency in Spanish was also positively related* to their performance on high school achievement tests in English, though the degree of relationship was less than that found between judgments of proficiency in English and scores on achievement tests in English.

Results such as the foregoing suggest that academic skills are related to overall skill in using either English or Spanish.

One interesting result cited suggests that frequency of oral use of Spanish at home between students and parents was a negative predictor of Hispanics' high school achievement. Given the results just discussed, there is the possibility that intervening variables such as low socioeconomic status of family, low level of parental education, and recency of family migration to the U.S. mainland may be associated with frequency of use of Spanish at home and with children's low achievement in school. For example, recent Hispanic immigrant families may be relatively poor, insecure socioeconomically, and also more likely to use Spanish as the language of oral communication at home. In such families, Spanish spoken at home may not be accompanied by extensive literate practice of Spanish at home. Under such circumstances, given the absence of familiarity of students with English, it is understandable how more frequent oral use of Spanish at home could associate negatively with Hispanic students' high school achievement.

Findings cited in this chapter also indicate that the quality of classroom interactions for Hispanic children may be poorer than for Anglo children. Specifically, evidence was cited that teachers may have lower academic expectations and lower social esteem for Mexican American children than for Anglo children. The language background of Hispanic children has an indirect effect on school achievement as well as a direct effect. The direct effect is that children who are less familiar with English than other children profit less from instruction in English due to low proficiency in English. The indirect effect—which may be just as educationally devastating as the direct effect—is that teachers may have lowered expectations and esteem for Hispanic children whose English shows influence of the Spanish language.

A cursory examination of sociocultural and socialization factors possibly affecting Hispanics' school achievement suggests that teachers' stereotypical beliefs about cultural attributes of Hispanics could lead to teachers' lowered educational expectations of Hispanic children relative to their expectations of Anglo children. Research on Hispanic children's socialization, particularly on how Hispanic mothers and Anglo mothers teach their children to think, suggests that educational attainment level of parents, and not ethnicity, is the prime factor underlying children's learning of thinking and literary skills that help them accommodate to school.

While not explored in depth, Hispanics' propensity to adopt strong values in the strength and well-being of the family and community may on occasion have an unintended negative impact on schooling achievement. As cited earlier, Hispanic high school students are more likely than Anglo students to judge that matters of familial well-being affect schooling achievement. Given that: a) the socioeconomic well-being of Hispanic families is often below that of Anglo families; and b) that Hispanic children are more likely than Anglo children to be concerned with their families, it is possible to understand how in some circumstances Hispanic high school children are more likely than Anglo children to have events at home affect their schooling negatively. This negative effect seems to reflect the inability of schools to accommodate to the problems children face at home, rather than to reflect on the inappropriateness of Hispanics' cultural values.

One area that has not been touched on in this chapter, and that is likely to be of substantial importance in understanding Hispanic high school students' achievement, is the self-concept and personal educational aspirations of Hispanic children and the impact of these factors on school success. The research reviewed in this chapter suggests that Hispanic students face formidable barriers in reconciling the characteristics of their socioeconomic and linguistic cultural backgrounds with their educational experiences. The psychological and sociocultural barriers that Hispanics face in developing high educational aspirations, social integration into the American school system, and strategies for access to educational opportunities are probably not well understood except as the reality they are to those who must suffer the burden. In light of the research reviewed in this chapter, the foregoing comment suggests the importance of listening carefully to the advice and judgment of Hispanic students about their own educational concerns. Further suggested is the need for broader survey research on the self-concept and educational aspirations of Hispanic high school students. These issues will be explored in more detail in Chapter 6.

A final conclusion to be drawn is that more needs to be understood about how high school institutional factors, such as teacher selection and teacher training, counseling resources for students, racial and socioeconomic integration of schools, and general school finances, affect Hispanics' educational attainment. While not focusing on the foregoing issues, evidence cited in this chapter suggests that adequate high school resources, a hospitable high school social climate, and sensitivity of high school staff to Hispanics' background characteristics may be critical in optimizing Hispanic students' school achievement and preparation for college.

4

Hispanic College Admissions
Test Scores

This chapter surveys recent data compiled by the American College Testing Program and the College Entrance Examination Board on mainland Hispanics' college admissions test performance. It presents descriptive summaries of test performance of white non-Hispanics and of Hispanics broken down by Hispanic subgroup membership. The purpose of the material presented in this chapter is primarily descriptive, with minimal consideration of the factors underlying levels of test performance. For the College Board data that will be presented, it is possible to some extent to examine the relationship of test score differences to students' language background. This relationship provides evidence that needs consideration, clarification, and further exploration in further research on the prediction of students' college achievement.

The appendix of this report, "Testing of Hispanics' Cognitive Skills," is made available here as a brief survey of previous research on testing of Hispanics. While only a summary, the appendix is self-contained and should be of value to persons uninformed in this area.

AMERICAN COLLEGE TESTING
PROGRAM DATA

The American College Testing Program (ACT) college admissions standardized test is composed of four subtests in the areas of English, mathematics, social studies, and natural sciences. Each subtest provides a corresponding standardized score for examinees ranging from a minimum standard score of 1 to a maximum standard score of 36. In addition to subtest scores, a composite score ranging in value from 1 to 36 is computed on the basis of subtest scores. The scores on subtests are hypothesized to measure college candidates' developed academic abilities in an area. The composite score thus reflects candidates' overall potential for college achievement across basic subject matter areas.

For a thorough discussion of the design, purposes, and validation procedures of the ACT admissions testing program, see American College Testing Program (1973).

Table 13 presents 1978–79 ACT test average scores for candidates classified into three groups: Mexican American or Chicano students, Puerto Rican or Spanish-speaking American students, and Caucasian American/white students. The data presented are available in the publication, *College Student Profiles: Norms for the* ACT *Assessment, 1980–81 Education* (American College Testing Program, 1980).

Before discussing the ACT test score data presented in Table 13, it is essential to note that the data are based only on those institutions participating in the ACT Class Profile Service. For these institutions, the data represent a random sampling of 10 percent of all those students

Table 13

Mean ACT Scores and Standard Deviations for Representative Samples of Hispanic and Caucasian American/White Students

Group	ACT Subtest				
	English	Mathematics	Social Studies	Natural Sciences	Composite
Mexican American or Chicano students	14.1	12.6	12.5	16.6	14.1
Sample (N = 931)	(5.2)	(6.7)	(6.5)	(5.9)	(5.2)
Puerto Rican or Spanish-speaking American students	14.5	13.7	14.0	17.5	15.1
Sample (N = 190)	(5.6)	(7.3)	(7.2)	(6.2)	(5.8)
Caucasian American/white students	19.1	19.0	18.7	22.4	19.9
Sample (N = 34,172)	(4.9)	(7.3)	(6.9)	(6.0)	(5.4)

NOTE: Sample sizes given arise from a 10 percent random sampling of the full population of examinees in 1978–79 who enrolled in college as freshmen in 1979. Parentheses enclose standard deviations.

SOURCE: *College Student Profiles: Norms for the ACT Assessment,* 1980–81 edition. Iowa City, Iowa: The American College Testing Program, 1980, pp. 90–91, 93.

who took the ACT test in 1978–79 and who were admitted as freshmen to college in 1979. The particular sample sizes associated with each ethnic group category shown were those that happened to occur among the ten percent sample drawn. Ethnic classification of students was determined by responses to the ACT student questionnaire: The ACT Interest Inventory and Student Profile Section.

Inspection of the mean scores and standard deviation of ACT scores given in Table 13 shows that Caucasian American/white students outperformed the two Hispanic groups by about one standard deviation unit on all subtests and on the composite test score. Given the consistency of this result, the similarity in standard deviation of scores for all groups, and the size of the samples represented, it is clear that the differences in test scores between Hispanics and white non-Hispanics are real and of interpretable significance. The data of Table 13 reveal little difference among ACT scores for Hispanic students classified as Mexican American or Chicano and students classified alternatively as Puerto Rican or Spanish-speaking American.

The Student Profile Section of the questionnaire filled out by ACT examinees includes a single language background question, "Is English the language most frequently spoken in the home?" The ACT program literature cited in this report presents no evidence on the relationship of Hispanics' ACT scores to responses to this question.

COLLEGE ENTRANCE EXAMINATION BOARD DATA

The Admissions Testing Program (ATP) of the College Board uses the following tests: the Scholastic Aptitude Test (SAT), the Test of Standard Written English (TSWE), and currently 13 separate achievement tests in various areas of scholastic undergraduate training. When the tests are administered, students also fill out a background and educational aspiration questionnaire known as the Student Descriptive Questionnaire. The nature, purpose, research, and services of the College Board are described in a series of publications that are given in the catalog, *The College Board Publications, 1982–83* (College Board Publications, 1982). The Information Bulletin that is provided to students who apply for administration of tests carries full descriptive summaries of the nature, purpose, and format of tests. All data presented here are College Board data for 1979–80, cited with permission.

The SAT test is composed of two sections: the verbal section and the mathematics section. Both sections are intended to measure developed ability in use of language and in simple mathematical reasoning as might be expected of students in undergraduate college course work. According to the College Board (1980, p. 8):

SAT-verbal and SAT-mathematical scale scores range from 200 to 800. Both scales were established in the early 1940s and were arbitrarily defined to have a mean of 500 and a standard deviation of 100. Candidate performance on all subsequent editions of the SAT has been reported in terms of these base scales, but mean scores for current groups are below 500 and standard deviations tend to be somewhat above 100.

Table 14 displays mean verbal and mathematics SAT subtest scores for Mexican American, Puerto Rican, and white examinees in 1979–80. Information on ethnic identity was obtained by voluntary responses to an item on the Student Descriptive Questionnaire. Table 14 also gives standard deviations and sample sizes for each respective ethnic subgroup and subtest. Inspection of the summary data of Table 14 reveals that white non-Hispanic students showed a 70-point advantage over Mexican Americans on the verbal section and an 86-point advantage over Puerto Ricans on the same section. On the mathematics section, white non-Hispanics averaged a score that was 69 points higher than

Table 14

Scholastic Aptitude Test (SAT) Mean Scores 1979–80 for Hispanics and Non-Hispanic Whites

Group	Verbal	Mathematics
Mexican Americans	372 (S = 101) (N = 14,169)	413 (S = 104) (N = 14,167)
Puerto Ricans	356 (S = 102) (N = 6,849)	387 (S = 104) (N = 6,848)
Whites	442 (S = 103) (N = 720,010)	482 (S = 111) (N = 719,891)

NOTE: Standard deviations (S) are given in parentheses along with sample sizes (N).

SOURCE: College Entrance Examination Board Data, 1979–80.

Mexican Americans and 95 points higher than Puerto Ricans. The discrepancy between white non-Hispanics' performance and Hispanic subgroup performances thus ranges from about two-thirds to one standard deviation standard score unit in favor of white non-Hispanics. This difference is meaningful to interpret given the similarity in the standard deviations of subscores for all groups. Overall, the pattern of differences in college aptitude scores is consistent with the findings in the case of the ACT test of the American College Testing Program, though the differences appear slightly smaller in the case of the College Board SAT test.

Discussion will next be given to 1979–80 ATP results on the Test of Standard Written English (TSWE). The TSWE College Board test is a thirty-minute multiple-choice test that is administered with the SAT. To quote the College Board on design of the test (ATP Guide for High Schools and Colleges 1979–81, p. 4):

> The TSWE evaluates students' ability to recognize standard written English, the language of most college textbooks and the one they will be expected to use in the papers they will write for most college courses. The scores are not intended to be used by a college in making admissions decisions but are meant to help place students in appropriate freshman English courses.

Scores on the TSWE test range from 20 to 60+, the latter score assigned for all scores 60 and above. Given the nature of the TSWE, scores on this test might be expected to be sensitive to students' language background, especially in cases where students show more familiarity with a non-English language than familiarity with English. In the case of such a language background pattern, Hispanics' performance on the TSWE might be depressed accordingly, due to characteristics of TSWE performance that stem from greater familiarity with the Spanish language. However, it could also be the case that TSWE scores do not simply and necessarily reflect direct language interference from a non-English language to English. For example, as mentioned in an earlier chapter, bilingual background examinees may develop styles and norms for English usage that do not conform to standard norms for English writing but do conform to social expectations for written usage of English among persons from a similar bilingual or monolingual community background.

Table 15 displays TSWE scores from 1979–80 for Mexican American, Puerto Rican, and white non-Hispanic examinees. The mean TSWE score of white non-Hispanics was 44.3, which represented an advantage of 6.6 points over the average score for Mexican Americans and an ad-

Table 15

Test of Standard Written English (TSWE) Mean Scores for Hispanics and Non-Hispanic Whites, 1979–80

Group	Mean TSWE score	Standard deviation	N
Mexican Americans	37.7	10.6	14,167
Puerto Ricans	35.2	10.7	6,850
Whites	44.3	10.1	719,972

SOURCE: College Entrance Examination Board data, 1979–80.

vantage of 9.1 points over the average score for Puerto Ricans. The standard deviation of TSWE scores was highly similar across Hispanic and white non-Hispanic groups. The TSWE score differences constituted roughly a one-half to one standard deviation advantage in TSWE score units in favor of white non-Hispanics over Hispanics. The magnitude of advantage was very similar to the magnitude of advantage of white non-Hispanics over Hispanics on the SAT-verbal and SAT-mathematics subscores.

Available College Board data on Hispanics' SAT scores and on one question of the Student Descriptive Questionnaire (SDQ) do permit investigation, if only in a limited sense, of how Hispanic students' language background is associated with SAT performance. Question 38 on the SDQ asks: "Is English your best language?" to which a multiple-choice response of "Yes" or "No" can be selected. Table 16 gives median SAT-verbal and SAT-mathematical scores for Mexican American, Puerto Rican, and white non-Hispanic SAT examinees, organized by the response of "Yes" or "No" to Question 38.

The data given in Table 16 are interesting in several respects. For purposes of understanding the comparisons that follow, first note that the data for the white non-Hispanic group in Table 16 are restricted to those white candidates that answered "Yes" to SDQ Question 38. Presumably, those whites who answered "No" are more likely to represent persons whose native language is not English or persons who have resided away from the U.S. English-speaking populace extensively.

Second, note that the percentage of Mexican American and Puerto Rican examinees taking the SAT who indicated English was their best language exceeds 90 percent of the responses to Question 38 in the case

Table 16

Hispanic and White Non-Hispanic SAT **Verbal and Mathematics Median Scores in Relation to Answers about English as Best Language (1979–80, SDQ Question 38)**

Group	SDQ Question 38 response: English as best language	Percent of a group	Median SAT verbal score[2]	Median SAT mathematics score[2]
Mexican Americans	Yes	93.1	368	404
N = 14,048[1]	No	6.1	290	350
Difference in medians to Yes/No responses			78	54
Puerto Ricans	Yes	90.2	351	374
N = 6,779	No	9.8	283	334
Difference in medians to Yes/No responses			68	40
White, non-Hispanics	Yes	98.2	436	479
N = 716,460	No	1.8	352	434
Difference in medians to Yes/No responses			84	45

[1] N is based on those examinees who responded to SDQ question 38 *and* who had an SAT verbal section score.
[2] Median scores rather than mean scores are reported since available tabulations reviewed used only median statistics.

SOURCE: College Entrance Examination Board data, 1979–80.

of both groups. If the meaning of the SDQ question is interpreted conservatively by Hispanics, "Yes" responses to Question 38 identify students who judge they communicate better in English than in a non-English language; however, note that such "Yes" responses do not necessarily indicate that English is used with the same proficiency or range of fluency as would likely be the case for native speakers of English. It is an open possibility that some "Yes" responses to Question 38 come from Hispanics who are better at speaking English than Spanish but who might nonetheless manifest a lower level of standard English proficiency than white non-Hispanic candidates.

The difference in median scores on the verbal SAT subtest and the mathematics SAT subtest for English-dominant versus non-English-dominant Hispanic examinees is in the expected direction, and this difference is slightly larger for the verbal score than for the mathematics score. The median verbal and mathematics scores of Hispanics who answered "Yes" to the question, "Is English your best language?" were lower on both subtests than was the case for white non-Hispanics who answered "Yes" to the same question. The differences represent about one-half to one standard deviation in SAT score units.

Further discussion on use of candidate questionnaires, such as the SDQ, as a means for investigating background factors mitigating interpretation of SAT scores, TSWE scores, or scores on other admissions tests in predicting college performance of Hispanics is given in a later chapter. Consideration is given to the possibility of using an augmented version of existing instruments such as the SDQ or ACT Student Profile to tap more sensitively language and other background characteristics of Hispanics that might moderate use of college admissions test scores and high school grades in predicting college performance.

While this report is concerned primarily and centrally with issues surrounding prediction of Hispanics' *undergraduate* college performance, it is insightful to consider information on Hispanics' graduate college admissions test performance. The Graduate Record Examinations Aptitude Test (GRE) of the Graduate Record Examinations Board measures students' developed ability in three areas related to graduate education: verbal, quantitative, and analytical ability. The three subscores on the GRE Aptitude Test were scaled originally to have means of 500 and standard deviations of 100, with a score range of roughly from 200 to 800 depending on the subtest. Drawing on data in the publication, *A Summary of Data Collected from Graduate Record Examinations Test-Takers During 1978–79* (Wild, 1980), Table 17 displays mean verbal, quantitative, and analytical ability scores in 1978–79 for self-identified Mexican American, Puerto Rican, Latin American, and white non-Hispanic students. Ethnic classification of examinees was based on responses to a background questionnaire administered to examinees. The category "Latin American" represents students who described themselves as "other Hispanic or Latin American," given the other Hispanic alternatives of Puerto Rican or Mexican American/ Chicano.

The data given in Table 17 show that, compared to white students, all three groups of Hispanic examinees on the GRE Aptitude Test attained lower mean scores on every GRE Aptitude subtest. Overall, it appears that Mexican American and Puerto Rican Hispanics scored

Table 17

Mean GRE Aptitude Test Scores and Standard Deviations for Self-Identified Hispanic and White Non-Hispanic Examinees, 1978–79

	Group			
GRE **Aptitude Subtest**	**Mexican American**	**Puerto Rican**	**Latin American**	**White**
Verbal	418.82	389.42	464.97	511.50
	(109.51)	(104.69)	(113.14)	(110.52)
Quantitative	422.14	417.71	467.72	525.08
	(122.27)	(119.93)	(125.81)	(121.96)
Analytical	412.26	384.70	460.27	528.73
	(116.61)	(111.70)	(125.31)	(110.61)

NOTE: Standard deviations are in parentheses.

SOURCE: Wild (1980, p. 75).

about one standard deviation below whites; Latin Americans scored about a one-half standard deviation lower in performance than whites.

CONCLUSIONS AND DISCUSSION

The data reviewed in this chapter have shown that Hispanic college candidates' admissions test scores were from one-half to one standard deviation below the scores of white non-Hispanics. These differences were found to exist on the undergraduate admissions tests of both the American College Testing Program and the College Board, and also on the subscores of Graduate Record Examinations Board Aptitude Test. Mexican American (or Chicano), Puerto Rican, and other Hispanic candidates performed at levels very similar to each other and noticeably lower than whites. On the College Board Student Descriptive Questionnaire, Mexican American or Puerto Rican students who answered "Yes" to the question, "Is English your best language?" scored higher by about one standard deviation on the SAT-verbal and SAT-mathematics subtests than Mexican or Puerto Rican students who answered "No" to the same question. The SAT scores of Mexican

American or Puerto Rican students who answered "Yes" to the question, "Is English your best language?" still scored more than one-half standard deviation below white non-Hispanics who answered "Yes" to the same question on both the SAT-verbal and SAT-mathematics subtest.

The Test of Standard Written English (TSWE) scores of Mexican American and Puerto Rican students averaged between one-half and one standard deviation below the TSWE scores of white non-Hispanics.

Under the assumption that the admissions test scores of Hispanics are valid indicators of students' college aptitude, one is led to the inescapable conclusion that Hispanic college candidates are not as prepared academically for college work as white non-Hispanic students. This conclusion seems totally consistent with other evidence brought forth earlier in this report regarding Hispanics' high school achievement patterns.

The foregoing conclusion needs to be tempered by consideration of several factors. First, there is the very real possibility that the admissions test scores of some Hispanics are depressed by factors that do not represent developed academic ability per se, but that do affect test score performance. For example, greater familiarity with Spanish than English, when coupled with a strong educational background in Spanish, may lead to lower Hispanic admissions test scores in English than are indicated based on students academic ability in Spanish. Other factors affecting test performance spuriously and perhaps linked to language may reflect performance demands and test-taking strategies that block Hispanic students from doing as well on tests as they otherwise might be capable of doing. Four such factors that are discussed in a limited fashion in the next chapter include: guessing, test anxiety, test speededness, and familiarity with vocabulary on tests.

A second source of factors influencing Hispanics' depressed level of admissions test performance undoubtedly resides at a more distal level in the lower socioeconomic and educational attainment level of Hispanic families. While not addressed here, there is little question but that Hispanics' admissions test scores would average lower as the socioeconomic level of parents decreases. The fact that this relationship exists for all students regardless of ethnicity is indicative of the real educational advantages of families who are better off socioeconomically. The evidence cited earlier in Chapters 3 and 4 is consistent with this conclusion. However, it is important to note that it is not socioeconomic level of families in itself that might directly cause admissions test score performance. As discussed previously, the educational experiences of Hispanics are mediated more directly by familial and school experiences that affect Hispanics' effective participation and performance in school. One important corollary of this caveat is that it allows the possibility that educational and social intervention on behalf of Hispanic students, where desirable, might work to improve Hispanics' educational achievement and preparation for college. Increases in college admission test scores of Hispanics then might become a gauge by which to evaluate the effectiveness of providing Hispanics with more equitable educational experiences.

The next chapter goes on to review studies using high school grades and college admissions test scores to predict Hispanics' college grades. The chapter also reviews selected studies investigating other factors that may affect Hispanics' college aptitude and achievement test performance.

5

Predictive Validity and Population Validity Studies

This chapter reviews empirical research studies investigating the validity of high school grades and admissions test scores in prediction of Hispanic college students' grades. The chapter is divided into two parts. The first part reviews publicly available studies that used regression analysis methods or correlational methods to establish associations between college grades as a criterion variable and high school grades and college admissions test scores as predictor variables. Most, but not all, of the studies discussed in the first part address the question of population validity. In the present context, the population validity issue is whether prediction of college grades from high school grades and admissions test scores remains invariant in pattern of prediction and accuracy across ethnic populations. The populations investigated include Anglos and Hispanics and sometimes blacks.

With one exception, research reviewed on use of regression and correlational analyses in prediction of U.S. mainland Hispanics' college grades from high school grades and college admissions test scores is on Hispanics who are most likely Mexican Americans. This chapter also includes a very brief overview of a series of predictive validity studies conducted in Puerto Rico. Interpreted cautiously, the latter studies suggest just how well college grades in a total Spanish speaking environment might be predicted from high school grades and performance on a Spanish-version college admissions test. Discussion of one Mexican predictive validity study is also included, although this study relied on a locally developed admissions test.

Following the review of population and predictive validity studies, discussion is given to a major synthesis of the outcome of most of these studies in a more general work by Breland (1979). The findings of the present review are compared with the findings of the Breland synthesis.

The second part of this chapter briefly reviews other studies of Hispanics' admissions test performance or collegiate scholastic ability. Attention is given to interrelationships among different admissions test performances of Hispanics and the possible influence of English-language proficiency on test performance in English. Attention is also given to test item characteristics or examinee characteristics that may lead to differences in test performance between Hispanics and Anglos.

The concluding section of this chapter summarizes what was learned from reviewed studies and sets the stage for the last chapter of the report, which discusses needed research on enhancing prediction of Hispanics' college achievement given background issues reviewed in this report. Readers not interested in learning the details of the studies reviewed in this chapter may find it beneficial to proceed to the concluding section of the chapter.

REGRESSION AND CORRELATIONAL STUDIES OF PREDICTIVE VALIDITY AND POPULATION VALIDITY

The treatment provided in the description of studies is not intended to provide a thorough or comprehensive statistical discussion of the use of regression techniques in population validity studies. For a detailed discussion of the use of regression methodology in population validity studies, the reader is referred to the work of Breland (1979), Olmedo (1977), and American College Testing Program (1973). The objective of the review of studies given here is to inform readers of the findings of empirical research on predictive and population validity issues concerning prediction of Hispanics' college grades. In the review, no attempt is made to discuss alternative statistical models and other approaches to prediction of college grades, unless such models or approaches are investigated empirically in the studies cited.

Regression and Correlational Analysis Studies of College Grade Prediction: U.S. Hispanic Students

All of the studies reviewed in this section are described in detail in public documents; they appear as papers published in journals or else appear as dissertations.[8]

All of the studies summarized in this section, except the last, concern Hispanics who are most likely to be in the majority of Mexican Americans. This inference is based on information available in studies and on the basis of the location of institutions from which students were sampled.

Calkins and Whitworth (1974). The purpose of this study was to develop and contrast linear regression equations predicting freshman grade-point average from SAT-verbal scores, SAT-quantitative scores, and high school quartile rank. Four groups of students at the University of Texas at El Paso were studied: Spanish-surname females (N = 530), Spanish-surname males (N = 711), non-Spanish-surname females (N = 804), and non-Spanish-surname males (N = 1192). The students studied were drawn from all entering freshmen during the period fall semester 1969 to fall semester 1971; only students with complete data profiles were included. According to Calkins and Whitworth, the fact that the data of their study were collected at a time when the University of Texas at El Paso was following an essentially open admissions policy meant that their results were unusually free of restriction in the ranges of the academic and test score variables they examined.

Calkins and Whitworth were careful to note disadvantages in the criterion and predictor variables they chose to examine. They indicated that quartile rank in high school was chosen as a criterion variable because it was the only data on high school achievement that was available, despite its imprecision as an indicator of high school achievement. Use of freshman grade-point average was judged a disadvantage because it was not necessarily comparable across subject areas that varied in intrinsic academic difficulty. Finally, determination of ethnicity or cultural background by surname was felt to be insensitive to students' actual heritage and their degree of acculturation to Anglo culture. The data on which the study was based showed that Spanish-surname students averaged lower scores than non-Spanish-surname students on all academic achievement and academic aptitude measures.

Correlations between SAT-verbal and freshman grade-point average were .34 for Spanish-surname females, .25 for Spanish-surname males, .37 for non-Spanish-surname females, and .32 for non-Spanish-surname males.

Correlations between SAT-quantitative and freshman grade-point average were .28 for Spanish-surname females, .23 for Spanish-surname males, .34 for non-Spanish-surname females, and .33 for non-Spanish-surname males. SAT composite scores correlated .35 with freshman grade-point average for Spanish-surname females; the other respective correlations were .27 for Spanish-surname males, .40 for non-Spanish-surname females, and .38 for non-Spanish-surname males.

High school quartile rank correlated with freshman grade-point average at a level of −.34 for Spanish-surname females, −.36 for Spanish-surname males, −.38 for non-Spanish-surname females, and −.42 for non-Spanish-surname males. The negative correlations described here reflected a positive relation between high school rank and freshman GPA, since the high school quartile rank used "1" as an index of highest ranking and "4" as an index of lowest ranking.

The results of regression analyses predicting freshman GPA for all groups indicated that a composite of SAT subscores and high school quartile rank predicted 17 percent of freshman GPA variance for Spanish-surname females, 15 percent of freshman GPA variance for Spanish-surname males, 22 percent of freshman GPA variance for non-Spanish-surname females, and 23 percent of freshman GPA variance for non-Spanish-surname males. Statistical significance tests questioning whether the weights estimated for the same predictor variables across groups were equal were conducted. The results showed that there were only minor statistically nonsignificant differences in the importance of SAT scores and high school quartile rank as predictors of freshman GPA across ethnic and gender groups. A statistical test of the equivalence of the intercept term in regression equations across gender and surname groups (using estimates of weights for predictor variables based on pooled data) revealed that the intercept value was significantly higher for females than males, regardless of Hispanic- or non-Hispanic-surname group membership. This result suggested that females' freshman grade-point average would be underpredicted by a composite of SAT and high school quartile rank measures based on pooled gender data. Calkins and Whitworth (1974) concluded that they had not found statistical grounds for advocating the use of separate regression prediction systems for Hispanic-surnamed versus non-Hispanic-surnamed students. The research showed that overall Hispanic students attained lower freshman grade-point averages, commensurate with their lower SAT scores and lower high school achievement rankings relative to non-Hispanic students.

Calkins and Whitworth did not devote extensive discussion to differences in the magnitude of correlations between SAT subscores, high school achievement rankings, and freshman grade-point average across Hispanic-surnamed and non-Hispanic-surnamed students. Their results, outlined earlier, indicated that SAT subscores tended to be correlated noticeably lower with freshman grade-point average for Hispanic-surnamed males and females than for non-Hispanic-surnamed males and females.

Goldman and Richards (1974). This research investigated prediction of college grade-point average from SAT-verbal and SAT-mathematical subscores among Mexican American and Anglo American students at the University of California at Riverside. Research was divided into two studies. The first study involved entering freshmen in the fall of 1971 with complete data records for the variables under investigation and who had completed the winter quarter in the same school year. Second quarter GPA (based on a 5-point scale) was predicted from SAT-verbal and SAT-mathematics scores for the two groups, which were identified as Mexican American by surname (N = 42) and Anglo American (N = 210). Anglo American students were randomly sampled from registrar records. Statistical analyses of group differences on mean GPA, SAT-verbal, and SAT-mathematics scores were significant, with Anglo American students manifesting higher mean scores on all measures. SAT-verbal scores were found to correlate .40 with GPA for Anglo Americans and .33 for Mexican Americans. The correlation of SAT-mathematics scores with GPA was .37 for Anglo Americans and .12 for Mexican Americans.

Separate regression models were fit to data for Anglo American and Mexican American students, with winter quarter GPA as the criterion variable and SAT-verbal and SAT-mathematics as separate predictor variables. The statistical hypothesis that both groups could be described by the same regression plane was rejected using a method adopted from Wilson and Carry (1969). The multiple correlation coefficient for the Anglo American regression system was .44; the corresponding multiple correlation coefficient for Mexican Americans was not reported, though the comment was made that its value was not statistically significant from the multiple correlation coefficient for Anglo Americans.

Inspection of the separate regression equations for the two groups revealed that SAT-mathematics scores were statistically significant contributors to prediction of Anglo American GPA but not so for Mexican American GPA. SAT-verbal scores were significant contributors to prediction of GPA for both groups. When the Anglo American prediction equation was used to predict Mexican American GPA, the results showed overprediction of GPA for Mexican Americans (predicted average GPA = 2.66 versus obtained average GPA = 2.28).

A second follow-up study was conducted in the winter of 1973 based on use of the entire student body population of the University of California at Riverside. On this occasion, Mexican American vs. Anglo American ethnicity of students was determined by self-disclosure of students rather than researchers' classification of surname. Winter GPA was used as the criterion variable, and again, SAT-verbal and SAT-mathematics scores served as predictor variables in regression analyses for both groups. The total number of Anglo American students studied was 1700, while the total number of Mexican American students was 110. The mean GPA, SAT-verbal, and SAT-mathematics scores for Anglo American students were higher than the same mean scores for Mexican American students, though no statistical significance test of differences between means was reported.

Inspection of the separate prediction equations resulting from regression analyses for each ethnic group showed that Mexican Americans' actual grade-point average (actual GPA = 2.58) would be overpredicted (predicted GPA = 2.64) by use of the Anglo American prediction equation on Mexican American students. The multiple correlation coefficient between GPA and the optimal weighted combination of SAT-verbal and SAT-mathematics scores that best predicted GPA was .33 (p < .01) for Anglo Americans and .24 (p < .05) for Mexican Americans.

Interpretation of the weights estimated for SAT-verbal and SAT-mathematics scores in regression equations for both groups revealed, as in the previous study, that SAT-mathematics scores did not contribute significantly to prediction of Mexican American GPA, whereas SAT-mathematics scores contributed significantly to prediction of Anglo American GPA. However, SAT-verbal scores were statistically significant as predictors of GPA for both Anglo Americans and Mexican Americans in regression equations.

In their summation, Goldman and Richards concluded that SAT scores were useful predictors of Anglo Americans' and Mexican Americans' grades when incorporated as predictor variables in separate regression equations for both groups. However, in another result, it was noted that overprediction of Mexican American GPA arose from use of an Anglo American regression system for prediction of Mexican American GPA. Goldman and Richards did not devote much discussion to the fact that SAT-verbal and SAT-mathematics scores correlated less with GPA for Mexican Americans than for Anglo Americans.

Goldman and Richards discussed the hypothesis that cognitive style differences between ethnic groups accounted for the difference in the regression systems they found in their studies. According to cognitive style research, based loosely on the work of Castaneda, Ramirez, and Herold (1972), Goldman and Richards contended that "there is reason to expect Mexican American students to restructure abstract tasks so as to make them less impersonal. This might imply less use of mathematical or syllogistic reasoning" (p. 134); later they stated, "This hypothesis is suggested because field dependent individuals [i.e., Mexican Americans] are more 'comfortable' with 'humanistic' or 'pragmatic' reasoning than 'abstract reasoning.' " Goldman and Richards ruled out an alternative hypothesis that course selection patterns were responsible for the lack of importance of SAT-mathematics scores in predicting GPA for Mexican Americans, because school records allegedly did not reveal differences in major study areas for the Mexican American and Anglo American freshmen studied.

In concluding the review of the Goldman and Richards research, it is important to emphasize that their conjectures on cognitive style differences between Anglo American and Mexican American students were speculative; no research evidence for these conjectures for the actual school population studied were presented or cited.

The occurrence of bilingualism among Mexican Americans was mentioned in the introduction of the Goldman and Richards (1974) paper as a factor needing consideration in interpreting the validity of college entrance test score data as predictors of Mexican Americans' college grades; there was no follow-up to this concern evidenced anywhere in the body of the paper.

Goldman and Hewitt (1975). The purpose of this study was to test replicatability of the earlier work of Goldman and Richards (1974) on prediction of Mexican Americans' college grades, using a new set of institutions. The study also sought to include high school grade-point average (HSGPA) as a predictor of college grades in addition to SAT-verbal and SAT-mathematics subscores. Four universities from a western multi-campus state university were studied; these schools represented approximately 60 percent of the undergraduate enrollment in the entire state university system. Chicanos represented from 1 to 4 percent of enrollees at each institution sampled.

All students studied were Anglo or Chicano undergraduates enrolled in the four schools during the 1974 winter quarter. Ethnicity was based on each student's self-report. Only those students with complete college grade-point average (GPA), high school grade-point average (HSGPA), and SAT-verbal and SAT-mathematics data were studied. The number of Chicanos and Anglo Americans at each of the four university sites were, respectively: 261 and 5635; 84 and 5500; 180 and 2926; and 131 and 3127. Mean GPA, HSGPA, SAT-verbal and SAT-mathematics scores of Anglo American students were higher than corresponding measures for Mexican Americans at each of the four university sites. Correlations between HSGPA and college GPA for Anglo Americans ranged from .30 to .40, and for Mexican Americans ranged from .21 to .42. Correlations between SAT-verbal scores and college GPA for Anglo Americans ranged from .28 to .34, and for Mexican Americans ranged from .16 to .42. Finally, correlations between SAT-mathematics and college GPA for Anglo Americans ranged from .21 to .26, and for Mexican Americans ranged from .13 to .38. One university site for Mexican Americans seemed to show noticeably higher correlations between HSGPA, SAT-verbal, and SAT-mathematics measures, and college GPA than all other sites. Exclusion of this one site would have lowered the range and strength of correlations between college GPA measures and predictor measures for Mexican Americans. The new range of correlations would have been .21 to .37 for HSGPA correlated with GPA; .16 to .25 for SAT-verbal scores correlated with GPA; and .13 to .18 for SAT-mathematics scores correlated with GPA.

Separate regression analyses were conducted for each school site according to ethnic subgroup, with college GPA as the criterion variable and HSGPA, SAT-verbal scores, and SAT-mathematics scores as predictor variables. Statistical tests of parallelism of regression planes within school sites across Anglo American and Mexican American groups revealed that the college GPA prediction equations estimated for the two ethnic groups were significantly different at each of the four university sites. In interpreting these latter results, Goldman and Hewitt (1975) pointed out that the practical importance of these findings was trivial. In the case of the university site showing the greatest statistical discrepancy between prediction equations for the two ethnic groups, use of separate college GPA prediction equations for Anglo Americans and Mexican Americans would have only accounted for an additional .8 percent of variance in GPA variance totalled over both groups, over the use of a single regression equation. Goldman and Hewitt concluded that lack of need of separate regression equations for Anglo American and Mexican American groups was further reinforced by comparing the predicted versus actual Mexican American average college GPA at each school site using the Anglo American prediction equation derived for the same school site. The comparison procedure required substitution of the constant term estimated in the regression equation for Mexican Americans in place of the constant term in the prediction equation for Anglo Americans. The results of the subsequent analyses indicated that Mexican Americans' grades were predicted fairly well by the Anglo regression equations thus modified for each institutional site.

In discussing the predictive adequacy of the original regression equations they developed for each separate ethnic group site, Goldman and Hewitt did not comment on the values of the multiple correlation coefficient obtained for each regression equation. For Anglo Americans, the multiple correlation coefficients ranged from .41 to .48 over the four university sites, while the corresponding range for Mexican Americans was .28 to .49. If the university site with the highest multiple correlation coefficient for Mexican American students was excluded, the range of multiple coefficient values would have been from .28 to .37, which is much lower than the corresponding range of multiple correlation coefficients for Anglo Americans. These results suggested that, overall HSGPA, SAT-verbal, and SAT-mathematics scores were more accurate predictors of Anglo Americans' college GPA than of Mexican Americans' GPA.

One final set of analyses conducted by Goldman and Hewitt addressed how much more additional college GPA variance would be accounted for by including SAT-verbal and SAT-mathematics scores as college GPA predictors in addition to HSGPA scores in the same regression equations for each university site and ethnic group. The range of additional college GPA variance accounted for by adding in the predictive effect of SAT-verbal and SAT-mathematics scores was from 4 to 8 percent for Anglo Americans, and from zero to 6 percent for Mexican Americans. Goldman and Hewitt (1975) argued that these results suggested that SAT scores added very little to predicting college grade-point average for either ethnic group, beyond information already contained in high school grades. At the same time, Goldman and Hewitt (1975) pointed out the need for some type of instrument to predict Chicanos' college success more accurately, and they further indicated that use of less accurate methods than those currently in use could lead to damaging results, excluding otherwise qualified Chicanos from admission to college.

As part of the assessment of their findings, Goldman and Hewitt indicated that while their results did not show gross over- or underprediction of Mexican Americans' college GPA, there were still possible issues of bias in use of SAT subscores as predictors of college GPA, since Mexican Americans differed from Anglo Americans more on SAT subscores than on the criterion measure college GPA. Based on Thorndike (1971), this criticism stemmed from the issue that decisions about admission (rather than prediction of college grades) placed unequal emphasis on the importance of test scores across ethnic groups, in that "whatever factors are unique to the [admissions] test differentiate the two groups more sharply than the factors that are unique to the criterion [grade-point average]" (Thorndike, 1971, p. 67).

In the conclusion to their paper, Goldman and Hewitt raised three issues for further research. First, there was a need for replication of their work in state and private colleges, as well as two-year community colleges. Second, there was a need for research on the structure of cognitive abilities among Chicanos comparing this structure to the structure of cognitive abilities among Anglo Americans. And finally, there was research needed on design of better admissions test predictors of Chicanos' academic success. They suggested that an appropriate new test would place less stress upon understanding written English instructions. It was suggested that this de-emphasis of the importance of understanding test instructions might lead to better discrimination of underlying constructs measured by academic ability tests. This suggestion was founded on data in the study that showed higher intercorrelations among SAT-verbal and SAT-mathematics subscores for Chicanos than for Anglo Americans; these data supported the view that SAT-verbal and SAT-mathematics scores did not measure academic skills that were as separate for Mexican Americans as for Anglos. Goldman and Hewitt offered no substantive discussion of language abilities among Chicanos to support the conjecture they introduced.

In a final comment, Goldman and Hewitt introduced the issue that efforts to establish predictive validity of college achievement rested upon the validity of the college GPA criterion itself. This issue was not addressed at all in the body of the paper.

Lowman and Spuck (1975). Prediction of first-year college grade-point average and number of courses passed during the first year of college was studied for a group of 75 Mexican Americans. The 32 females and 43 males investigated were students in the period 1968 through 1970 enrolled in Claremont College, a private undergraduate college system in California. Students' Mexican American ethnicity categorization was based on surname. The study exclusively involved Mexican American students, some of whom were admitted to school under a special admissions program for students from disadvantaged backgrounds. The study sought to predict college achievement measures from traditional predictors (SAT-verbal and SAT-mathematics scores and high school grade-point average) and also from nontraditional (background) predictor measures representing low income level, English-language difficulty status, denial of regular college admissions status, and high IQ underachievement status. Separate analyses were conducted for female and male students. The nontraditional background variables were coded dichotomously in analyses, with "1" indicating existence of a trait and "0" indicating absence of a trait.

The results of the study showed that first-year college grade-point average for females correlated .319 with SAT-verbal scores, .275 with SAT-mathematics scores, and −.020 with high school grade-point average. For males, first-year grade-point average in college correlated −.080 with SAT-verbal scores, .203 with SAT-mathematics scores, and .409 with high school grade-point average. All but one of the correlations reported between first-year college grades and high school grades or SAT measures for males and females were statistically insignificant. The only correlation attaining statistical significance was the .409 correlation between first-year grade-point average in college for males and their high school grade-point average.

Among background predictor variables, English-language difficulty showed no significant correlation with first-year college grade-point average for both males and females; however, the variable English-language difficulty did show a significant negative correlation of −.376 with males' verbal SAT scores. Given the lack of numerically continuous background predictor variables in the study and low sample sizes involved, it is difficult to interpret sensibly the pattern of other correlations reported, since they were often of an opposing sign across male and female groups with no clear interpretation as to gender influences.

Prediction of college GPA from SAT-verbal, SAT-mathematics, and HSGPA variables alone by means of regression analyses did not attain statistical significance in separate analyses for males and females; the resulting R^2 statistics reported were .113 for females and .071 for males. Prediction of number of courses passed in the first year of college from SAT-verbal, SAT-mathematics, and HSGPA measures by means of regression analysis similarly did not attain statistical significance for both female and male groups; the resulting values of R^2 were .134 for females and .194 for males.

Regression analyses were also used to predict college GPA and number of courses passed in the first year of college separately for females and males from so-called nontraditional predictor background variables alone. These analyses excluded use of SAT-verbal, SAT-mathematics, and HSGPA measures, the latter labeled "traditional predictor variables." As mentioned earlier, the background variables were low family income, English-language difficulty, denial of regular college admission, and high IQ with underachievement. This second set of regression analyses led to statistically significant results in prediction of all criterion measures for both male and female groups. The value of R^2 for prediction of college GPA from a weighted combination of background variables was .455 for females and .281 for males. The value of R^2 for prediction of number of college courses passed from a weighted combination of background variables was .437 for females and .282 for males.

A third set of regression analyses investigated how well prediction of college GPA and number of first-year college courses passed could be improved by using background variables in addition to SAT-verbal, SAT-mathematics, and HSGPA measures as predictor variables in regression analyses. The results of the new analyses showed that increased prediction of college GPA variance was 12 percent for females and 4 percent for males; these increments in the corresponding R^2 statistic were statistically significant at $p < .05$. Also, the results of the new analyses showed that prediction of variance in the criterion variable — number of first-year college courses passed — was improved by 13 percent for females (p < .002) and 6 percent for males (p < .10) by adding in information about background variables to regression equations already allowing for SAT-verbal, SAT-mathematics, and HSGPA measures.

The results of the three sets of regression analyses discussed demonstrated that nontraditional predictor measures — background variables — were statistically more significant predictors of college achievement than traditional predictor measures, which alone were not statistically significant predictors of college achievement. The study also found that the level of prediction of college achievement was best predicted by including both traditional and nontraditional measures in regression analyses.

Goldman and Hewitt (1976). The purposes of this study were to investigate prediction of college GPA among a sample of black (N = 272), Asian (N = 852), Chicano (N = 188) and white (N = 4259) undergraduate students enrolled in the University of California system during the 1973–74 academic year. The students investigated were enrolled at the University of California at Los Angeles (UCLA), the University of California at Davis (UCD), the University of California at Irvine (UCI), and the University of California at San Diego (UCSD). Predictor variables included ethnicity category, major, HSGPA, and SAT-verbal scores, and SAT-mathematics scores. Ethnicity was determined by students' self-reports. Only students with complete data profiles were studied. The principal research questions were 1) Was college GPA prediction for Chicanos and Asians similar to prediction of college GPA for blacks and whites? and 2) Did major field of study mediate ethnic differences in test performance?

Multiple regression analyses were used on pooled data at each university site to determine how well college GPA could be predicted from ethnicity, major, HSGPA, SAT-verbal scores, and SAT-mathematics scores. Results of data analyses were most extensively discussed for one school, UCLA, with the claim that this manner of reporting was parsimonious. since the data and analyses given in the paper's tables for other schools essentially paralleled the findings at UCLA. At UCLA, ethnic differences were found in the criterion variable, college GPA; Chicanos had a GPA average of 2.65 as compared to a GPA average of 2.89 for whites, 2.81 for Asians, and 2.52 for blacks. Across all UCLA ethnic groups studied, ethnic group membership on its own accounted for two percent of the variance in college GPA. For the UCLA sample, inclusion of predictor variables representing HSGPA, SAT-verbal scores, and SAT-mathematics scores, in addition to ethnicity in regression equations predicting college GPA, boosted prediction of college GPA variance by 16 percent over use of ethnicity as the sole predictor variable in analyses.

Chi square analyses of students' choices of major area of study at the four universities investigated revealed that there was a significant statistical association ($p < .0001$) between ethnicity and major field. No breakdown of proportion of ethnic group members by area of study is provided in the paper. Regression analyses were conducted to determine whether or not prediction of college GPA would be improved by including ethnicity as a predictor variable, in addition to major as a predictor of GPA. For the UCLA data, the results showed that ethnicity predicted a little over two percent of GPA variance not already predicted by major area of study. Goldman and Hewitt concluded that these results suggested that ethnic differences in GPA at UCLA were not due simply to differences in choice of major field. Results from regression analyses from the other University of California campuses studied showed a similar finding.

For each ethnic group and campus site, a test of parallelism for college GPA prediction equations yielded statistical results implying that, except for UCLA, there were no major differences in prediction equations across ethnic groups at each site. Goldman and Hewitt (1976) concluded that for all practical purposes the regression systems used to predict college GPA for the separate ethnic groups could be considered parallel at each university site.

Further analyses of regression results showed that virtually all ethnic group differences in college GPA were explainable by ethnic group differences in HSGPA, SAT-verbal scores, and SAT-mathematics scores.

Inspection of correlation patterns between college GPA and the predictor measures of HSGPA, SAT-verbal scores, and SAT-mathematics scores showed that SAT-verbal and SAT-mathematics scores were more intercorrelated for blacks and Chicanos than for Asians and whites. This result was interpreted to account for the fact that multiple correlations of GPA with combined HSGPA, SAT-verbal scores, and SAT-mathematics scores were noticeably lower for blacks and Chicanos than for Asians and whites, thus implying that combined HSGPA, SAT-verbal scores, and SAT-mathematics scores were more valid predictors of Asian and white college GPA than they were of black and Chicano GPA.

As in their previous paper (1975), Goldman and Hewitt (1976) in the present study conjectured that blacks' and Chicanos' weakness in interpreting written instructions on the SAT-verbal and SAT-mathematics subtests could depress resulting subtest scores and lead to a higher than otherwise intercorrelation among these scores. As before, no discussion of linguistic issues was presented to substantiate this claim in more detail. The last section of the paper commented on ethical questions of unfairness raised by use of high school grade information and admissions test scores in the process of making admissions decisions. A little discussion was given regarding the "Thorndike procedure," which would eventuate in admitting minority applicants to college with lower HSGPA and SAT scores than nonminority applicants. It is mentioned that this latter procedure could be viewed as unfair to whites. Goldman and Hewitt (1976, p. 116) comment:

> The "solution" of simply eliminating educational tests is no solution at all. Even if no tests are used, admissions decisions must still be made, and the issue of unfair selection would continue to exist. These difficulties would be further compounded by lower validity of less-objective selection procedures.

A final comment by the authors mentioned the need for development of more discriminating predictors of college academic achievement for blacks and Chicanos. They suggest that such an accommodation could be brought about by simplifying instructions on the SAT, thereby improving interpretation of SAT scores, since performance on the SAT would then be less dependent on understanding instructions. The authors caution that misinterpretation of the findings of the work they presented could lead to the unwarranted conclusion that HSGPA and SAT scores were valid beyond question as predictors of minority students' college grades.

Warren (1976). In this work, sponsored by the College Entrance Examination Board, three campuses of the California state college system were selected for study. The objectives of the study were to compare the structure and statistical fit of regression equations for predicting college GPA for Mexican American and "other" category students. Analyses subdivided ethnicity groupings into male and female samples, or else pooled students without regard to gender. Three criterion GPA measures were involved in reported analyses: freshman GPA, sophomore GPA, and upper-division college GPA. Predictor measures included high school grades, and either the composite ACT or else a totaled SAT score. Separate analyses were conducted, depending upon whether ACT or SAT scores were to be entered into regression equations. The number of Mexican American subjects entering into analyses varied from 19 to 163, while the number of other category subjects varied from 43 to 250 in analyses. Other category students were randomly selected from non-Mexican-Hispanic comparison groups that matched Mexican American subjects by sex and year of college.

Results of descriptive data analyses showed that, regardless of gender, Mexican Americans earned lower college entrance test scores, lower high school grades, and lower college grades than did other category students at each campus.

Regression analyses were reported according to whether freshman GPA, sophomore GPA, or upper-division grades was the criterion variable. Analyses were also broken down according to whether ACT composite scores or, alternatively, total SAT scores were used as predictor variables along with high school grades. The results of analyses at three institutions showed, with the one exception for male groups at one institution, that prediction of freshman GPA from college entrance test scores and high school grades was no more inaccurate for Mexican American than for other category students. Comparison of the weights assigned predictor variables as a result of analyses indicated, with two exceptions, that there were no significant differences between Mexican American and other category students in the importance of high school grades and test scores as predictors of freshman GPA. The results of analyses also indicated, without exception, that there were no statistically significant differences between Mexican Americans' expected GPA and other category students' expected freshman GPA after accounting for the influence of admissions test scores and high school grades in predicting freshman GPA for both groups.

At the one institution where sophomore grades were studied, results of regression analyses using composite ACT scores and high school grades to predict sophomore college GPA showed no difference in the accuracy of prediction for Mexican American and other category students. In addition, there were no significant differences in the weights assigned composite ACT scores and high school grades in predicting sophomore GPA. Finally, the results of analyses showed no significant differences in the expected sophomore GPA of Mexican American and other category students after accounting for the influence of composite ACT scores and high school grades in predicting sophomore GPA.

The remaining set of regression analyses carried out by Warren considered prediction of upper-division college grades from college admissions test scores and high school grades at two college institutions. Regardless of whether composite ACT scores or total SAT scores were used along with high school grades as predictors, the results of analyses were consistent with the previous findings. As with the previous analyses discussed, no statistically significant differences were found in the accuracy of prediction of college grades for Mexican American and other category students. In addition, in only two of five analyses did differences arise in the weights assigned test scores or high school grades in predicting upper-division GPA. In two of three cases, there were also no significant differences in expected upper-division GPA between Mexican American and other category students after controlling for the influence of college entrance test scores and high school grades.

Warren concluded that his work did not support a hypothesis that different regression equations were needed to predict Mexican American versus other category students' college grades from high school grades and college entrance test scores. This conclusion was upheld by the results of regression analyses, despite the fact that high school grades correlated more strongly with college grades than did admissions test scores for both Mexican American and other category students. The conclusion was qualified by Warren because of the use of data that featured incomplete records for some students. A further qualification, not mentioned by Warren (1976), is the relatively low number of subjects entering into many analyses, which would possibly lead to unstable statistical results.

In discussing the results of his work, Warren commented on college admissions policy. He conveyed the idea that admissions test scores and high school grades ought not to be expected to carry the full burden of evidence for deciding college admission among students. Mention is made of institutional priorities relating to increasing minorities' access to college, which might guide colleges' evaluation of the importance of college candidates' college admissions test scores and high school grades.

An additional issue raised by Warren was that, in contrast to views which hold that college is intended for the best prepared, another view has received increasing attention. This latter view holds that society gains substantial benefits by having minority and low income students succeed in college, where previous information would suggest that such students would not be as academically qualified as other students based on traditional college achievement predictor measures.

Goldman and Widawski (1976). This study investigated the utility of high school grade-point average and SAT scores in prediction of average grade-point average among Anglo, black, and Chicano undergraduate students enrolled at UCLA, UC Davis, UC San Diego, and UC Irvine during the 1974 spring quarter. The first purpose of the study was to investigate the relative contribution of HSGPA and SAT scores to prediction of college GPA across various ethnic/racial groups and institutions. A second purpose of the study was to use "selection-outcome" matrices to investigate whether HSGPA or combined HSGPA and SAT scores would change the number of students from

Table 18

Amount of Variance on GPA Accounted for by HSGPA and SAT: Chicanos

College	N	HSPGA R^2	HSPGA + SAT R^2	R^2 increase
UCLA	263	.14	.14	.00023
UC Davis	84	.17	.24	.07
UCSD	180	.04	.06	.02
UC Irvine	129	.13	.13	.007

SOURCE: Goldman and Widawski (1976).

each ethnic/racial group that would be expected to achieve a hypo-thetical criterion grade-point average in college at each institution. Table 18 (Goldman and Widawski, 1976, p. 188) of this study shows the amount of variance in Chicanos' college GPA accounted for in regression analysis by use of HSGPA as a sole predictor variable or else by use of HSGPA and SAT as combined predictor variables in analyses.

On the basis of the results summarized in the table, Goldman and Widawski concluded that use of SAT scores added little to explain college GPA that could not already be predicted by HSGPA.

The outcome of the second part of the study, which was relevant to Chicanos, indicated that at each institution studied fewer Chicanos would have been admitted on the basis of a hypothetically required college GPA of 2.5, if both HSGPA and SAT scores were used to predict college GPA than if HSGPA had been used alone as a predictor of college GPA. To quote Goldman and Widawski (1976, p. 192): "Using a GPA = 2.5 success criterion, use of the SAT at the four universities would make inadmissible 15 percent, 12 percent, 14 percent, and 14 percent of Chicano applicants who would have been admissible through use of HSGPA alone." In interpreting this statement, the reader of this report is cautioned that the Goldman and Widawski analyses were not intended to describe how UC campuses actually select students. The Goldman and Widawski (1976) selection-outcome analyses were simulation analyses demonstrating how use of a predicted college grade cutoff point in deciding admissions would have been biased in admission of Chicanos to college.

Scott (1976). This work was a Ph.D. dissertation at the University of New Mexico investigating prediction of junior-year college grade-point average among Anglo (N = 878), black (N = 67), and Mexican American (N = 66) students. The predictor variables used were HSGPA and ACT composite scores. Correlations between Chicanos' college junior standing GPA with HSGPA were .26 and with ACT composite scores were .20. For Anglos, these correlations were respectively .31 and .21. The multiple correlation (R) between college junior GPA and combined HSGPA and ACT composite scores was .29 for Chicanos, while the corresponding R for Anglos was .32. Scott concluded that combined use of HSGPA and ACT composite scores led to a small but meaningful increase in prediction of Anglos' and Chicanos' grade-point average in the junior year of college beyond the level that would have been possible if only HSGPA had been used as predictor of college grades.

Use of the Gulliksen-Wilks procedure to compare regression parameters across Anglo and Chicano college GPA prediction equations led to the conclusion that the regression parameters were not statistically different for both Anglo and Chicano prediction equations. Results for blacks are not discussed here.

The Scott dissertation concluded with a set of recommendations for further research. As relevant to Chicanos, these suggestions included the need for: studies of differences between students who attained junior status in college and those who left college prior to junior standing; development of college grade prediction equations by academic area of study; use of other schooling and background variables to predict success in college; study of the effects of English-language proficiency on admissions test scores; and longitudinal prediction studies of college achievement, which include attention to a variety of criteria of college achievement extending beyond grade-point average.

Dittmar (1977). This work was a Ph.D. dissertation study at the University of Texas at Austin. The principal purpose of the study was to investigate equivalence of prediction regression equation parameters in prediction of college GPA from SAT scores, English Composition Test (ECT) scores, and high school percentile rank (HSR) for male and female Anglo, black, and Mexican American students at the University of Texas at Austin in 1974 and 1975.

The descriptive data concerning means and intercorrelations among measures shown in Tables 19 and 20 were reported for Anglos and Chicanos (data on blacks are here excluded). The data shown in Tables 19 and 20 are only for students who had ECT scores; other analyses in the study involved students regardless of availability of ECT scores.

Table 19

Means, Standard Deviations, and Intercorrelations of Predictor and Criterion Variables for Anglos Who Had Data Available on the ECT for 1974 and 1975

| | 1974 (N = 218) | | 1975 (N = 254) | | | | | | |
	Mean	S.D.	Mean	S.D.	HSR	SAT-V	SAT-M	ECT	GPA
HSR	78.72	16.56	78.17	18.45	—	.316	.382	.370	.487
SAT-V	517.89	90.60	506.57	90.43	.154	—	.570	.704	.421
SAT-M	556.47	85.35	549.37	99.11	.236	.572	—	.581	.439
ECT	505.83	94.52	510.47	101.79	.263	.756	.529	—	.432
GPA	2.89	.68	2.80	.78	.478	.378	.410	.475	—

NOTE: Correlations for the 1974 group are given above the diagonal; correlations for the 1975 group, below.

SOURCE: Dittmar (1977, p. 104).

Table 20

Means, Standard Deviations, and Intercorrelations of Predictor and Criterion Variables for Mexican Americans Who Had Data Available on the ECT for 1974 and 1975

| | 1974 (N = 187) | | 1975 (N = 266) | | | | | | |
	Mean	S.D.	Mean	S.D.	HSR	SAT-V	SAT-M	ECT	GPA
HSR	86.24	12.45	84.26	13.76	—	−.058	.102	.177	.216
SAT-V	445.24	89.40	440.68	88.42	.026	—	.420	.712	.361
SAT-M	493.05	83.43	496.09	78.15	.042	.223	—	.492	.349
ECT	446.74	87.26	460.34	85.62	.149	.711	.312	—	.438
GPA	2.72	.63	2.60	.77	.203	.157	.165	.369	—

NOTE: Correlations for the 1974 group are given above the diagonal; correlations for the 1975 group, below.

SOURCE: Dittmar (1977, p. 106).

While not discussed in much detail in the dissertation, the tables indicated that the ECT scores of Mexican Americans correlated more strongly with college GPA than other predictor measures. With Anglos, the correlation between ECT scores and college GPA exceeded the relationship between college GPA and SAT scores, but it was about the same as the relationship between college GPA and HSR scores.

Substitution of ECT scores for SAT-verbal scores in regression analyses predicting entering Mexican Americans' college GPA from HSR and SAT scores led to enhancement of the resulting multiple correlation coefficients; in the case of the 1974 sample, the change was from an R of .470 to .484; for the 1975 sample, the change was from an R of .283 to an R of .402. The same strategy of substitution of ECT for SAT-verbal scores in regression analyses for entering Anglo students showed a change of R from .582 to .579 for 1974 sample students, and a change from .591 to .616 for 1975 sample students.

Results of statistical significance tests to compare the regression equations for predicting college GPA for Mexican Americans and Anglos led to a finding of no significant differences among weights assigned predictor variables, and among mean square residuals from prediction. The results also showed that prediction equations derived for Anglo and Mexican American groups were of statistically significantly different structure from the regression equations for prediction of blacks' college GPA.

Other results of the study indicated that the use of a single regression equation for all students, regardless of ethnic classification, over the two school years studied would have led to slight overprediction of blacks' grades, slight underprediction of Anglos' grades, and accurate prediction of Mexican Americans' grades.

Mestre (1981). This study, conducted during the 1980 and 1981 academic years, investigated college GPA and word problem-solving skills of 60 undergraduate bilingual Hispanic engineering and science students and 73 English monolingual technical study area undergraduates. Students investigated attended a major eastern state university; no mention is made of the Hispanic subgroup origin of the students. The 60 Hispanic students were composed of 35 freshmen, 12 sophomores, 10 juniors, and 3 seniors. According to Mestre, all but 11 of the Hispanic students investigated were judged to be balanced bilinguals on the basis of nearly equivalent performances on Spanish and English versions of language proficiency examinations. The monolingual group was composed of 57 freshmen, 10 sophomores, and 6 juniors; 53 of these persons were engineering majors, and the remainder majored in science areas.

The predictor variables used in analyses included: 1) SAT-verbal and SAT-mathematics scores; 2) Test of Reading, Level 5, and Prueba de Lectura, Nivel 5 scores; 3) Test of General Ability, Level 5, Part III: Computation; 4) Formula Translation Examination and Traduccion de Formulas test scores; 5) Short Algebra Inventory English and Spanish test scores; and 6) Word Problem Inventory scores in English and Spanish. The Word Problem Inventory test in each language was developed at the investigator's institution. It consisted of simple arithmetical word problems that required examinees to understand the meaning of brief stretches of text in either language. Depending upon analyses, the Word Problem Inventory was used alternatively as a criterion or predictor variable.

Bilingual Hispanic students possessed lower average college GPA scores, SAT-verbal, and SAT-mathematics scores than monolinguals. Performance on all other tests in English was also lower for Hispanic bilingual students.

The results of correlational analyses indicated SAT-verbal scores correlated .12 with Hispanics' college GPA, and correlated .35 with monolinguals' college GPA. The SAT-mathematics scores correlated .42 with Hispanics' college GPA, and correlated .53 with monolinguals' college GPA. Interestingly, Hispanics' three subscores on the Prueba de Lectura, Nivel 5 Spanish reading comprehension test correlated higher with college GPA than SAT-verbal test scores did. For example, in the most extreme case, the Vocabulary subscore on the Prueba de Lectura test correlated .48 with Hispanics' college GPA. Hispanics' Test of Reading, Level 5 English reading comprehension test subscores correlated roughly at almost the same level with college GPA as did their corresponding Spanish reading comprehension test scores.

The subscores of monolingual students on the Test of Reading, Level 5 English reading comprehension test did not correlate noticeably as well with college GPA as did their SAT-verbal scores. Overall, for monolinguals, scores on the Short Algebra Inventory test, the Word Problem Inventory test, and the Formula Translation Examination test correlated almost as well with college GPA as did SAT-verbal scores, but not as well as did SAT-mathematics scores.

Regression analyses on Hispanic bilingual and monolingual groups were conducted, using either college GPA or scores in the English version Word Problem Inventory test as criterion variables. The analyses were conducted in a step-wise procedure with predictor variables introduced into analyses in their order of importance as independent predictors of criterion scores in regression analyses. The

SAT-verbal and SAT-mathematics scores were *not* included as predictor variables in regression analyses. The results of regression analyses indicated that Hispanic bilinguals' college GPA was most significantly predicted by scores on the Word Problem Inventory and the Vocabulary subscore of the Test of Reading, Level 5. In contrast, the most important predictors of monolinguals' college GPA were scores on the Formula Translation Examination test and the Short Algebra Inventory test. These results demonstrated that prediction of Hispanics' college GPA was more influenced by skills requiring English-language performance than was the case for monolinguals.

Prediction of Word Problem Inventory test scores showed that the Short Algebra Inventory test and Vocabulary subscore of the Test of Reading, Level 5 were the most important predictors of criterion performance for both Hispanic bilinguals and monolinguals.

Mestre concluded that his results demonstrated that Hispanic bilingual technical area students' GPA and mathematical skills were more correlated with English-language skills than was the case for English monolingual technical area students. Mestre concluded that SAT-verbal scores were not very valid predictors of Hispanic students' college GPA, despite the fact that only 26 of 60 Hispanics possessed SAT scores for investigation in the sample studied. This caveat regarding sample size seems to diminish the potential validity of Mestre's conclusions somewhat.

Breland's (1979) Synthesis of Population Validity Studies. Breland (1979) provided an extensive survey and synthesis of existing predictive validity and population validity studies involving prediction of college grades from admissions test scores and high school achievement records for Anglos, blacks, and Chicanos. All of the studies reviewed earlier in this section were included by Breland except for Lowman and Spuck (1975), Dittmar (1977), and Mestre (1981).

Table 21 displays median correlations between college predictor measures and college grades that occurred in the studies Breland reviewed. As shown in Table 21, median correlations between high school grades and college grades across studies Breland reviewed were .36 for Chicanos and .37 for Anglos. Median correlations between college grades and college entrance verbal test scores across studies Breland reviewed were .25 for Chicanos and .37 for Anglos. Median correlations between college grades and college entrance quantitative test scores were .17 for Chicanos and .33 for Anglos.

Adjustment of the median correlation statistics given in Table 21 to reflect additional data in the studies of Dittmar (1977), Lowman and Spuck (1975), and Mestre (1981) reviewed in this report showed some

Table 21

Median Correlations Between College Predictor Measures and College Grades[1]

	Group		
	Breland Review		This Review[2]
Predictor	White	Chicano	Hispanics
High school record (HSR)	.37(32)	.36(8)	.30(14)
Verbal test scores	.37(45)	.25(9)	.25(16)
Quantitative test scores	.33(45)	.17(9)	.23(16)
HSR and admissions test scores	.48(61)	.38(25)	.38(31)

[1] Number of independent analyses over studies is indicated in parentheses.
[2] Includes the same analyses in Breland (1979), plus additional results not cited in Breland but cited in new studies reviewed here.

SOURCE: Breland (1979, p. 38).

changes over the original Breland median correlations. Over the range of studies reviewed here, the median correlation between high school grades and college grades for Hispanics was found to be .30 on the basis of 14 independent analyses. The conclusion to be drawn is that high school grades are somewhat less accurate predictors of Hispanics' college grades than of white students' college grades. It must be kept in mind that this conclusion is based on only a few studies. In particular, four analyses from one study (Dittmar, 1977), which were not reviewed by Breland, principally account for differences in the median correlation between Hispanics' high school grades and college grades reported by Breland versus the figure reported here.

As shown in Table 21, Breland found that the median correlation between Chicanos' verbal admissions test scores and college grades and the median correlation between Chicanos' quantitative admissions test scores and college grades were lower than for whites. The results of the present review support the Breland finding, though quantitative admissions test scores were found to be slightly more related to college grades for Hispanics than Breland found. The results of the Breland review suggested that Chicanos' quantitative admissions test scores were less related to college GPA than Chicanos' verbal admissions test scores. The results of the present review suggest very little overall difference between the association of verbal or quantitative admissions test scores with college grades for Hispanic students.

As shown in Table 21, Breland's survey of predictive validity studies further found that a combination of high school grades and admissions test scores was more highly related to whites' college grades than to Chicanos' college grades. The results of the present review involving a few more studies than Breland considered is totally consistent with Breland's findings.

In interpreting the median correlations based on the Breland review and the present report as shown in Table 21, it is important to remind the reader that the number of independent correlational analyses considered for Hispanics is relatively small (ranging from 14 to 31 in the case of the present review). This suggests the need to identify and review the characteristics of other validity studies that might exist and also to carry out further predictive validity studies in order to reliably assess population correlations for the variables of Table 21. A further qualification in order is the fact that the Hispanic correlations analyzed possibly are influenced by larger variance among predictor and criterion variables than is the case for Anglos. This variation may arise from measurement error due to chance factors, from factors that bear some systematic relation to language and background characteristics of Hispanics, or from factors reflecting systematic variation in Hispanics' college experiences — e.g., course selection patterns and grading patterns.

Breland's (1979) overview of Chicano and Anglo predictive validity studies concluded that there was not convincing evidence that prediction of college grade-point average, by means of regression analysis involving high school grade-point average and college entrance test scores, differed dramatically for Chicano versus Anglo category students within the school sites studied. Breland held this to be the case both in terms of statistical analysis of differences in the estimates of the value of regression weights across regression equations for Anglo and Chicano populations, and in terms of patterns of over-prediction or under-prediction that resulted from attempting to use Anglo equations to predict Chicanos' college grade-point average. These conclusions seem consistent with the evidence reviewed here.

While gross differences in prediction equations themselves did not consistently occur in the studies reviewed, accuracy of college grade-point prediction using equations is still an issue in the studies reviewed by Breland and the additional studies reviewed in this report. In virtually every study reviewed, the proportion of college grade-point average variance predicted by means of regression equations was lower for Hispanic than for Anglo students, even when ethnic-specific regression equations were used. As shown in Table 21, Breland and this report found a median multiple correlation of .38 between college grades and combined test scores for Chicano samples in contrast to a median multiple correlation of .48 for Anglo samples for the studies Breland reviewed. At present, the preliminary evidence seems to indicate that Anglos' college grades might be predicted about 9 percent more accurately than Hispanics' (principally Mexican Americans') college grades from high school achievement information and college admissions tests.[9] The implications of this disparity are discussed in later portions of this report.

Regression and Correlational Analysis Studies of College Grade Prediction: Puerto Rico and Mexico Studies

The studies reviewed in this next section concern prediction of Puerto Rican or Mexican students' college grades in a Spanish-speaking environment.

Predictive Validity Studies in Puerto Rico. The studies briefly noted here all involve use of the Prueba de Aptitud Academica (PAA), which is a Spanish version of the SAT test developed for use in Puerto Rico by the College Board. Development of the PAA involves an identical methodology as used with the SAT, though PAA test contents reflect knowledge and use of standard written Spanish. Previous research describing a process by which PAA subscores are equated with SAT scores is described in Angoff and Modu (1973).

Predictive validity studies carried out for client colleges and universities in Puerto Rico by the College Board Office in Puerto Rico use PAA-verbal and PAA-mathematics scores along with high school grade-point average to predict first-year college grade averages. Table 22 displays ranges and median correlations between first-year college grades and PAA subscores and high school grade-point averages for studies carried out at 10 Puerto Rican colleges and universities over the period 1968–69 through 1978–79.[10] Schools and individual data are not given to preserve their anonymity.

Comparison of the median correlations for Puerto Rico given in Table 22 of the association between predictor measures and college grade-point average demonstrates a noticeable resemblance to similar correlations given in Table 21 for whites in the United States. The median correlations between Puerto Ricans' PAA-verbal and PAA-mathematics subscores and college grade-point average are noticeably higher

Table 22

Range and Median Correlations of PAA Subscores and High School Grade-Point Average with First-Year College Grade-Point Average (1968–69 to 1978–79): 10 Sample Puerto Rican College Institutions

Predictor	Range	Median correlation
PAA-verbal	.26–.44	.36
PAA-mathematics	.18–.48	.36
Mean high school grade-point	.29–.48	.405
All predictors combined	.42–.60	.525

SOURCE: Unpublished data of the College Board, Puerto Rico Office.

(as shown in Table 22) than the median correlations between Hispanics' verbal and quantitative admissions test scores and college grades (as shown in Table 21). Finally, note that the correlation of combined PAA admissions test scores and high school grades for Puerto Ricans correlates even slightly higher with Puerto Ricans' college grades than is the case for the corresponding correlations of combined admissions test scores and high school grades with college grades for U.S. mainland whites (the latter is shown in Table 21). These results suggest that use of a Spanish-language college admissions test with Hispanic native Spanish speakers can predict college grades as accurately as can admissions tests in a mainland U.S. context with a monolingual, nonminority population.

A Mexican Predictive Validity Study. In a recent paper entitled, "The development and validation of an entrance examination in a Mexican university," Alvidres and Whitworth (1981) mentioned that they found no previously published research on the use of college entrance examinations in Mexico in their review of educational research literature. It should be noted that their search for such studies appears to have been limited to research published in the United States or otherwise available through the ERIC clearinghouse system. In their own research, Alvidres and Whitworth (1981) studied the prediction of 292 freshmen's GPAs at the Universidad Autónoma, Chihuahua, Mexico, in the fall 1978 semester. The predictor variables included: scores on a college entrance examination constructed locally by Universidad faculty; "preparatoria" (college preparatory high school) GPAs; Beta IQ scores; and various interview ratings of examinees. Table 23 repro-

Table 23

A Step-wise Multiple Regression Analysis Predicting the University GPA (Variable 14)

Variable number and designation	R	R²	Increment in R²	Regression weights (B)	Zero order validity coefficient r
Entrance exam-math	.360	.130	.130	.285	.360
Preparatoria GPA	.402	.161	.031	.140	.231
Entrance exam-English	.416	.173	.012	.078	.265
Sex	.428	.183	.010	.114	.156
Entrance exam-geography	.436	.190	.007	.081	.157
Beta IQ	.440	.194	.004	−.064	.026
Interview-cultural	.442	.195	.001	.059	.183
Entrance exam-sociology	.443	.196	.001	.027	.101
Interview-social	.444	.197	.001	−.025	.123
Interview-vocational	.444	.197	.0003	.019	.119
Interview-personality	.444	.197	.0002	−.017	.110
Entrance exam-Spanish	.444	.197	.00003	.007	.224
Entrance exam-history	.444	.197	.00000	.000	.149

SOURCE: Alvidres and Whitworth (1981).

duces the results of a step-wise multiple regression analysis predicting university GPA, and it also displays zero order correlations between university GPA and each predictor variable.

The results of the regression analysis showed that inclusion of three predictor variables — Entrance Exam-Math, Preparatoria GPA, and Entrance Exam-English — accounted for about 17 percent of the variance in university freshman GPA; the corresponding multiple correlation coefficient that was obtained using these three variables was $R = .416$. Addition of all remaining predictor variables to the regression analysis increased the freshman GPA variance accounted for by only 2.4 percent. No reason is given in the description of the study for why Entrance Exam-Spanish scores, which correlated .224 with university freshman GPA, were entered into analyses only late in step-wise analyses.

The Alvidres and Whitworth (1981) paper does not discuss language of instruction at the Universidad Autonoma, Chihuahua. Presumably this language is Spanish, though students might be expected to read English for some course work. The .416 multiple correlation between freshman GPA and a linear combination of Preparatoria GPA, Entrance Exam-Math, and Entrance Exam-English compares favorably with multiple correlations between U.S. Anglos' college GPA and combined high school GPA and entrance examination test scores.

OTHER STUDIES OF HISPANICS' COLLEGE APTITUDE TEST PERFORMANCE

The present section presents a quick review of some other studies that investigated the suitability of college entrance examination test scores as predictors of Hispanics' college or high school achievement. With one exception, the studies cited are not predictive validity studies with grades as a criterion variable; their focus is on factors affecting the interpretation of Hispanics' and other minorities' college admissions test performance and on constructs measured by various types of test scores.

Rock and Werts (1979). This study investigated the hypothesis that SAT-verbal and SAT-mathematics subtest scores were measuring the same underlying cognitive factors across samples of Native American, black, Mexican American, Puerto Rican, Asian, and white samples of examinees. Roughly 500 examinees from each population were randomly sampled. Using analysis of covariance structure methodology to study the structure of correlations among subtest parts, Rock and Werts (1979) established that while ethnic/racial groups manifested different mean levels of test performance, and occasionally different reliabilities on test measures, the overwhelming statistical evidence supported the hypothesis that items on SAT-verbal and SAT-mathematics sections were measuring the same performance skills (in the same units of measurement) across ethnic/racial groups. The results for Mexican Americans, Puerto Ricans, and whites did not show marked differences in the reliabilities of SAT-verbal and SAT-mathematics subscores across groups, though one analysis of reliabilities seemed to show that whites' scores on the Test of Standard Written English (TSWE) were slightly less reliable than scores for Mexican Americans or Puerto Ricans.

Rock and Werts (1979) found evidence that both Mexican American and Puerto Rican examinees performed at levels more similar to whites on the mathematics SAT subtest than on the verbal SAT subtest.

Rock and Werts (1979) suggested that Hispanic (along with Asian) examinees' non-English-language background may be responsible for lower levels of attainment on the verbal section of the SAT test. Study of performance levels on one verbal type of item — analogies — showed that Puerto Rican examinees performed more poorly on this item than they were expected to. Rock and Werts suggested that Puerto Ricans' lack of familiarity with English may be the reason they did not perform as well as other groups on analogies items.

Breland and Griswold (1981). This study compared performance on seven College Board academic tests across gender and ethnic/racial identity groupings of examinees. The results of the work discussed here only pertain to comparisons between Hispanics (N = 445) and whites (N = 5, 236). The academic test scores compared were: SAT-verbal, SAT-mathematics, Test of Standard Written English (TSWE), and four subtest scores on the English Placement Test (EPT). The four EPT subtests were EPT-reading, EPT-sentence construction, EPT-logic and organization, and EPT-essay. The emphasis of the study was on describing how strongly EPT-essay scores could be predicted from SAT and TSWE scores.

Hispanics' EPT total scores correlated .74 with TSWE scores, .78 with SAT-verbal scores, and .52 with SAT-mathematics scores. Whites' EPT total scores correlated .68 with TSWE scores, .68 with SAT-verbal scores, and .40 with SAT-mathematics scores. Correlations of EPT subscores with TSWE, SAT-verbal, and SAT-mathematics scores each resembled very much the same pattern of correlations just reported for Hispanics' and whites' EPT total scores.

The results of regression analyses showed a multiple correlation R = .84 between Hispanics' EPT total score and combined TSWE, SAT-verbal, and SAT-mathematics scores. For whites, the corresponding R that was obtained was .75 in the same analysis. Comparison of regression equation predictions of EPT subtest scores from TSWE, SAT-verbal, and SAT-mathematics scores suggested that Hispanics' scores were somewhat overpredicted by use of a regression equation developed for whites. Other results of the study suggested that Hispanics who scored in the lower half of the TSWE score range wrote fewer high quality essays on the EPT-essay test than whites who also scored in the lower half of the TSWE score range. Another result suggested that Hispanics who scored high on EPT subtests other than the EPT-essay test did not write essays of as high a quality as expected based on other EPT subtest scores; this result was in contrast to the higher quality of essays of persons who scored high on other EPT subtests overall.

Alderman (1982). This study investigated prediction of 384 island

Puerto Rican college candidates' scores on SAT-verbal and SAT-mathematics tests from scores on the Prueba de Aptitud Academica (PAA), English as a Second Language Achievement Test (ESLAT), and Test of English as a Foreign Language (TOEFL). The purpose of the study was to investigate how proficiency measures in English moderated prediction of SAT subscores from corresponding subscores on the PAA of the same type as SAT subscores. The hypothesis under investigation was that prediction of SAT subscores from corresponding PAA subscores would be moderated by examinees' greater familiarity with Spanish over English.

A series of step-wise regression analyses was conducted that predicted SAT-verbal or SAT-mathematics scores from corresponding PAA subscores of the same type. TOEFL, ESLAT, or TSWE subscores were introduced singly into regression analyses in a second step and improvement in prediction of SAT scores from PAA scores was noted. In a third regression step, an interaction term between a PAA score and a TOEFL, ESLAT, or TSWE score was introduced into regression analysis, and the improved prediction of SAT scores was subsequently noticed and tested for statistical significance.

The results of step-wise analyses showed that prediction of SAT-mathematics or of SAT-verbal scores from PAA-verbal or PAA-mathematics scores was significantly improved when TOEFL or ESLAT English proficiency test scores were introduced singly as predictor variables in regression equations. Inclusion of an interaction term between PAA scores and a single English proficiency measure in regression equations improved predictability of SAT-verbal or SAT-mathematics scores even further, and at a statistically significant level of improvement over use of separate predictor terms for PAA and English proficiency measures alone. The results of regression analyses investigating prediction of SAT scores from PAA scores using TSWE scores led to detection of a significant moderator effect only in the case of prediction of SAT-verbal scores.

The results of the Alderman research provide empirical backing to the view that assessment of some Hispanic students' college aptitude in English may be moderated by their familiarity with the English language. These results must be interpreted cautiously. Alderman's subjects were island Puerto Ricans who had received extensive schooling in Spanish; these subjects had also had some exposure to English in Puerto Rican school systems. The background characteristics of many U.S. mainland Hispanics is very different from the Hispanics in Alderman's study. It could be the case that Alderman's findings about how

English proficiency skills moderate assessment of Hispanics' English-language college aptitude might hold only for U.S. Hispanics who are relatively low in basic English proficiency and who have had extensive exposure to Spanish in their schooling. Empirical research is needed in order to investigate these and other issues surrounding the influence of language background on assessment of U.S. Hispanics' English-language college aptitude.

Boldt (1969). This study was somewhat similar to the recent work of Alderman *(1982),* though it involved a different population and purpose. In 1967, 140 Dade County, Florida, junior and senior Spanish-English bilingual high school students were administered PAA and SAT tests, along with a student background questionnaire that included language items. The goals of the study were twofold: 1) to develop and compare PAA-based and SAT-based regression equations for predicting concurrent high school GPA, and 2) to determine whether measures of students' orientation to Spanish or English, or measure of students' socioeconomic status, could be used to augment prediction of GPA based on SAT and PAA scores.

Performance of some students judged stronger in Spanish than in English was higher on the PAA than SAT, and the results suggested that developing procedures for differential weightings of PAA and SAT scores in predicting GPA might improve predictability of GPA. Actual attempts to implement differential weighting of SAT and PAA tests did not lead to a significant improvement in prediction of high school GPA over use of the SAT-mathematics score alone. Boldt cautioned that his suggestions for differential weighting of SAT and PAA scores to predict grades might not be appropriate for students with strong Spanish proficiency skills and strong preference for Spanish use. In this latter case, he suggested use of the PAA over SAT to estimate GPA. Note that the Boldt work did not involve prediction of students' grades in college, but rather involved concurrent prediction of high school grades from PAA and SAT scores of Hispanic high school students.

Evans (1980). This study investigated the effects of altering time-per-section permitted on verbal or mathematics subtests constructed to resemble the SAT. The study sought to determine whether 20-, 30-, or 40-minute time limits per section would lead to different patterns of performance among black, Chicano, and white juniors in 12 high schools in urban and rural settings. All students who were studied planned to attend college. Only findings relevant to comparing Chicanos and whites are discussed here. Results of the study showed that Chicanos performed in a *speeded* fashion on a verbal subtest when allowed a "standard" time of 30 minutes to work items. A speeded effect occurs when examinees are unable to complete items on a test within a preset time limit. Whites did not show a speededness effect when allowed 30 minutes for the same subtest. Both Chicanos and whites showed evidence of a speededness effect when allowed only 20 minutes to work verbal subtests. The speededness effect was not present when both groups were allowed 40 minutes to work a test.

On the mathematics subtest, Chicanos' and whites' performances showed a speeded effect when performances occurred at 20- and 30-minute time limits. Analyses of performance on the mathematics test showed that Chicanos were less likely to solve items correctly the later that items occurred in a test as time to work on a test decreased. This result, which also occurred for blacks, led Evans to hypothesize that minority examinees might be employing poor test-taking strategies since whites did not show a similar performance effect.

Pike (1980). This work investigated possible guessing strategies among a sample of 1974 GRE Aptitude examinees who were classified by gender or ethnic/racial background (white, black, or Chicano). All gender and ethnic/racial background groups were matched in terms of average GRE Aptitude scores. Various statistical indicators in Part One of the study were used to estimate whether or not groups were performing at a better-than-chance level on verbal and mathematics test items. Performance on items was evaluated in terms of the items' position on tests and omission of previous items prior to working a current item. Part One of the study revealed only one difference across groups on measures representing possible occurrence of guessing strategies. The one significant finding was that Chicano females were more prone to omit working test items than all other groups.

Part Two of the study investigated how well small samples of white, Chicano, and black examinees performed problem-solving subtasks that were implicated in the solution of various types of verbal and mathematics items that might occur on the GRE Aptitude Test. No evidence was found that Chicanos' depressed performance stemmed from sources other than lack of knowledge of the skills required to solve mathematics problems.

Rincon (1979). This Ph.D. dissertation study at the University of Texas at Austin investigated the role of test anxiety and test speededness on performance on the School and College Ability Tests (SCAT). The subjects were 101 Mexican American and 80 Anglo American high school juniors. The SCAT was administered under a speeded (regular 20-minute time limit) condition or a power (40-minute time limit) condition. Subjects' test anxiety was assessed by scores on a factor representing the dimension of anxiety on an instrument known as the Test Anxiety Scale.

The results of the study showed that, for Anglo Americans, higher levels of test anxiety uniformly resulted in lower test performance regardless of time condition, while higher test performance was associated with less test anxiety. In the case of Mexican Americans, test speededness was found to debilitate test performance at low to moderate levels of anxiety but facilitated performance as level of test anxiety increased beyond the moderate range. That is, speededness-related aspects of test performance were moderated by Mexican Americans' level of test anxiety, a personality dimension. Thus, a personality dimension interacting with ethnic identity was more productive in predicting performance differences on the aptitude test in question than was ethnic grouping alone.

Sinnot (1980). Performance on the Graduate Management Admissions Test (GMAT) was studied in order to isolate factors that might make test items more difficult than on the average for female, minority, or foreign candidates than for white males who were native to the United States. Items that showed more difficulty on the reading comprehension, problem solving, and practical business judgment sections of the test were identified according to language background and ethnicity/race or gender classifications of examinees experiencing greater difficulty.

Relative to other language classifications, examinees from a Spanish-speaking background showed very few (at most one or two) items per subtest that were of special difficulty for their language background group but not for other language background groups.

Hispanic (Puerto Rican, Mexican American, and other Hispanic) examinees' performance, analyzed independent of language background, showed lower item completion rates on subtests than was the case for whites on all GMAT subtests. Hispanics' subtest performance did not lead to identification of more than one or two items per subtest that appeared more difficult to answer correctly for them than for other ethnic groups as a whole.

Speakers of Japanese, Chinese, and Indo-Iranian languages, and black women, showed the most prevalence of high numbers of unexpectedly difficult items across tests. Overall, Hispanics or speakers of Spanish did not find large numbers of items across subtests extraordinarily difficult relative to the number of highly difficult items encountered by examinees from all backgrounds as a whole. Nonetheless, Hispanics and speakers of Spanish found more items of high difficulty than whites who were native to the United States.

CONCLUSIONS AND DISCUSSION

The material reviewed in this chapter was divided into two parts. The first part of the chapter reviewed studies using regression analysis and correlational analysis to investigate the association of Hispanics' college grades with high school grades and college entrance examination test scores. The second part of the chapter reviewed miscellaneous studies investigating performance of Hispanics on college aptitude and college admissions tests. The emphasis of the studies reviewed in the second part of the chapter was on performance factors or background factors that might lead to difference in performance patterns across Hispanic and other ethnolinguistic groupings of examinees.

The main conclusion to be drawn for the first series of studies reviewed is that high school grades and admissions test scores were not as good predictors of U.S. Hispanics' college grades as they were of white non-Hispanics' college grades. Overall, the evidence indicated that there was less association between Hispanics' high school grades and college grades than there was for whites' grades. U.S. Hispanics' verbal and quantitative test scores did not associate as strongly with college grades as was the case for whites. The results of regression analysis (or alternatively multiple correlation analyses) showed that combined use of high school grades and test scores to predict Hispanics' college grades was roughly nine percent less accurate than use of the same procedure to predict whites' college grades. In some studies, there was evidence that admissions test scores contributed extremely little to prediction of Hispanics' college grades that was not already predicted by information contained in high school grades. The foregoing comment is not a general conclusion since, overall, the results of other studies reviewed support a conclusion that admissions test scores contributed to prediction of Hispanics' college grades.

In interpreting the validity of the conclusions cited above, it is essential to note that only a relatively few published studies or publicly available dissertation studies exist on prediction of Hispanics' college grades from high school grades and college admissions test scores. The low number of publicly available studies that can be analyzed in a review such as this one may lead to conclusions that would not be supported had more studies been reviewed. Clearly, there is a need to review other studies, some of which are not in the public domain, and a need for more research to provide reliable and valid evidence on the trends reported here. However, enough evidence appears to exist to suggest that some personal and background characteristics of U.S. Hispanics may moderate the relationship of high school grades and college admissions test scores in prediction of college grades in a way that is special to U.S. contexts and the use of English in the United States. White non-Hispanic students are undoubtedly a more socioculturally and linguistically homogeneous group than Hispanics residing in the U.S. The relationships between Hispanics' high school grades and college admissions test scores with college grades could be influenced by the degree to which Hispanics resemble the acculturation and language background of white non-Hispanics. Other factors in the background of Hispanics, such as socioeconomic well being of family and the educational background of parents, could also moderate the utility of high school grades and college admissions test scores in predicting college grades. In addition, the college experiences of Hispanics and the characteristics of colleges may also affect prediction of college grades based on college admissions test scores and high school grades.

The second part of the present chapter reviewed miscellaneous studies of factors possibly affecting Hispanic students' college aptitude test performance. Results from several studies suggested that Hispanics' familiarity with the variety of English used on admissions tests can affect test performance; however, this conclusion was not always supported. With the exception of a few studies, the effects of familiarity with English as a factor influencing test performance were not studied directly, and as a result, there is only limited information on how language background or language proficiency may actually affect test performance. It is worthwhile to review findings of three studies that identify important issues. Clear evidence for the impact of familiarity with English on college aptitude test performance was provided in the results of a study by Alderman (1982) involving island Puerto Rican college candidates. This study found that SAT test scores were more strongly related to scores on the PAA (the Spanish version of the SAT) when the influence of native Hispanic examinees' proficiency test scores in English was taken into account. The Alderman research findings verify that we can expect other Hispanics' test performance to be affected by familiarity with English. The results of a study by Mestre (1981), although based on small samples of subjects, also supported the conclusion that English-language skills figure prominently in Hispanics' aptitude test performance. Since there is considerable diversity in the language background of U.S. Hispanics and their literate fluency in both Spanish and English, the findings of Alderman's and Mestre's research may not be replicated exactly among all U.S. Hispanics.

Research findings of Breland and Griswold (1981) indicated that English essays of some Hispanics may be rated at lower levels of performance than expected, based on Hispanic examinees' scores on an objective English writing test. Results of this sort suggest that there may be subtle language background influences that affect some Hispanic college candidates' display of English skills on tests requiring writing. This hypothesis would seem to be consistent with sociolinguistic research findings discussed in a previous chapter, though detailed research on Hispanic college students has yet to be accomplished. The review of survey research on Hispanics' educational achievement and educational attainment also verified that language background may affect Hispanics' academic performance in English. The evidence cited in this chapter supports the conclusion that language background also may affect Hispanics' test performance.

Results of other research studies on Hispanics' college aptitude test performance indicated that speededness of tests and level of test-taking anxiety may affect test performance. Test speededness refers to the failure of examinees to complete all the items on a test because of time limits for testing. Results from two research studies (Evans, 1980, and Pike, 1980) indicated that Hispanics' performance on speeded tests was lower on some occasions than performance of whites. A study by Rincon (1979) found that level of test anxiety interacted with testing time limits in its effects on Mexican Americans' test performance. The Rincon results suggest that interactions among factors affecting test performance may occur for Hispanics in ways not resembling effects occurring for non-Hispanics. Familiarity with English used on tests adds another factor that may interact with speededness and anxiety level, but this issue has not been investigated.

Sophisticated methodological attempts to establish whether or not college admissions test scores are measuring the same abilities among examinees from different U.S. ethnic minority and majority backgrounds supported the conclusion that admissions test items overall were measuring the same skills across ethnic populations. In addition, studies inquiring whether examinees from different ethnic backgrounds used different strategies in working test items—independent of skill level—did not find evidence to support a conclusion that Hispanics followed different problem-solving strategies than white non-Hispanics in working test items. However, no studies have been done showing what explicit problem-solving strategies Hispanics use in solving college admissions test items as a function of their English language proficiency. For a discussion of other research on this issue, see the Appendix. It is likely that the issue of cultural influences on strategies used in solving admissions test items is far from settled. To date, no sophisticated studies using methods and models from cognitive psychology, psycholinguistics, and cross-cultural psychology have investigated Hispanics' problem-solving performance on college aptitude tests.

As a final note to this chapter, it is necessary to point out and highlight the conclusion that the evidence on prediction of Hispanics' college grades from high school grades and admissions test scores suggests that the latter information should be used with extreme caution in the admissions process. While evidence is still relatively sparse, the direction and pattern of findings thus far suggest that neither high school grades nor admissions test scores alone or in combination ought to bear the sole burden of evidence for making decisions to admit Hispanic-background students to college. The evidence reviewed in this study supports the positive value of high school grades and college admissions test scores in aiding decisions about Hispanics' college admission. However, the results suggest that admissions officers ought to rely critically on the overall profile of Hispanic students in making admissions decisions. The results of studies reviewed here suggest that admissions personnel need to be provided with a broader range of information on Hispanics' background, language, and culture in weighing admissions decisions. This view is consistent with research findings on college candidates' personal qualities as an aid to admissions decisions (Willingham and Breland, 1982). As will be discussed in the next chapter, concern for institutional characteristics and resources, students' school experiences, students' personal values and attitudes, and alternative indices of Hispanics' achievement in college may also be needed to improve prediction of Hispanics' success in college.

The next chapter summarizes the previous issues and finding of this report. It also introduces other student and institutional characteristics potentially affecting achievement and the definition of achievement. The chapter then goes on to suggest an agenda of needed research on prediction of Hispanics' college achievement.

6

Synthesis of Issues and Directions for Research

The first part of this chapter highlights some of the major findings concerning Hispanics' educational attainment and prediction of college achievement discussed in earlier chapters. The second part of the chapter introduces additional issues of basic importance in understanding Hispanic students' achievement in college. The additional issues include: the personal aspirations and qualities of Hispanic students; institutional factors and college experiences affecting prediction of Hispanic students' college achievement; and alternative ways of characterizing college achievement, as a supplement to grades. The final part of the chapter outlines some components of a research agenda for improving prediction of Hispanics' college achievement from the perspective of a college admissions testing program.

Before beginning the substantive discussion of this chapter, it is essential to recognize that much of this report has centered primarily on Hispanics gaining admissions to four-year colleges and universities, though the discussion of demographic and background characteristics has had wider generality. In many ways, the population of Hispanics attaining entry into four-year institutions is unrepresentative of the general Hispanic population of college age. It is also the case that well over half of Hispanics who attend college attend two-year institutions. These caveats must be kept in mind in the synthesis of issues and directions for research that follow, since the comments offered here pertain primarily to Hispanics admitted to four-year institutions or else aspiring to be admitted to four-year institutions.

SYNTHESIS OF ISSUES

Chapter 2 of this report, concerned with general demographic and background characteristics of U.S. Hispanics, revealed that educational attainment among Hispanics was lower than that for U.S. whites, and that level of educational attainment was linked to background factors reflecting parental and family income, educational attainment of parents, recidivism in schooling, and proficiency in English. Survey data and achievement test data from major national studies on Hispanics' high school achievement reviewed in Chapter 3 indicated that Hispanics, regardless of subgroup identity, received lower high school grades and scored lower on achievement tests than whites in all content areas of school assessed. Analyses of background and schooling factors associated with Hispanics' achievement in high school revealed that, in addition to factors already mentioned, worries about family welfare, parents' lack of interest in children's education, lack of availability of study space at home, and teachers' unresponsiveness to students' classroom contributions were associated negatively with Hispanics' high school achievement. Survey data cited in Chapter 3 further indicated that Hispanics who did complete high school and went on to college were more likely to attend two-year institutions than were white students, and that Hispanics were more likely to be part-time students in two-year colleges than were white students. Another finding indicated that Hispanics were two and one-half times less likely than non-Hispanics to obtain their bachelor's degree after four years of college study. In light of other issues mentioned earlier, the latter finding suggests the possibility that prediction of Hispanics' achievement in terms of traditional predictor measures may be affected by some of the same background factors that moderate educational achievement prior to college entrance. However, the effects of such moderating factors in Hispanics' college achievement remain to be clearly established and understood through intensive empirical research.

The influence of Hispanics' language background and proficiency in English and Spanish on schooling attainment and schooling achievement based on educational survey data is complicated to interpret. Evidence from survey data indicated that more frequent reliance on a non-English language over English was allied with lower educational attainment. However, some recent evidence from a national educational achievement study suggested that judgments of high proficiency in either Spanish or English associated positively with high school achievement. Other evidence cited in the same study suggested that preference for Spanish in oral interaction with family members was associated negatively with scores on achievement tests in high school; of course, the latter relationship is not necessarily a causal one.

College Board data for 1979–80 and American College Testing Program data for 1978–79 reviewed in Chapter 4 showed that Hispanics' college admissions test scores averaged about one-half to one standard deviation below college admissions test scores of white non-Hispanics. The College Board data revealed that Hispanics who indicated that English was not their best language attained lower SAT-verbal and SAT-mathematics scores than Hispanics who indicated English was their best language. The SAT-verbal and SAT-mathematics scores of Hispanics who indicated English as their best language were nonetheless lower than white non-Hispanics who indicated English was their best language.

A sample of published studies investigating prediction of Hispanics' college grades from high school grades and college admissions test scores reviewed in Chapter 5 indicated that, overall, Hispanics' college grades were predicted 9 to 10 percent less accurately than whites' college grades from combined high school grades and college admissions test scores. The results of the studies reviewed provided no consistent, strong evidence indicating that Hispanics' college grades were overpredicted versus underpredicted using prediction equations developed for white non-Hispanic college students (or else for students as a whole at the institutions studied). The reviewed evidence was also consistent with a hypothesis that prediction of Hispanics' college grades from high school grades and college admissions test scores is mitigated by background factors.

The second section of Chapter 5 reviewed studies investigating factors that influenced Hispanics' college admissions or college aptitude test performance. The results of the studies reviewed indicated that proficiency in English, speededness of tests, and test anxiety were factors affecting Hispanics' admissions test performance detrimentally in a manner not occurring with whites' test performance. Several studies found that Hispanics' and whites' performances on admissions tests (or instruments resembling college admissions tests) were indistinguishable except for the lower average scores of Hispanics. In the studies reviewed, no convincing evidence was found that Hispanics followed fundamentally different problem solving strategies in solving test items; however, extensive research on this issue has not been conducted.

In the previous chapters, some evidence has been presented that Hispanics' background, high school achievement, and college access are related to Hispanic subgroup identity. Specifically, some of the findings suggested that Cuban Americans outperformed all other Hispanic subgroups on high school achievement tests, and that Cuban Americans were more likely to enter college than other Hispanic subgroups. At present, it is impossible to ascertain what features, if any, of a Cuban American background—beyond socioeconomic status and parental education level—contribute to Cuban Americans' higher educational attainment relative to other Hispanic subgroups. The fact that Cuban Americans maintain the highest usage rates of Spanish and the most intensive Spanish-speaking background among Hispanic subgroups suggests that familiarity with a non-English language is not a necessary hindrance to Hispanics' educational attainment. Familiarity with Spanish and use of Spanish need not be connected with low English-language proficiency and inability to succeed in school. However, some bilingual education research suggests that eventual success in English-language schooling may require or be aided by bilingual schooling. This is conjectured to hold for all Hispanic subgroups and for all Hispanic subgroup persons who show more familiarity with Spanish than English.

Intrinsic variation among Hispanic subgroups, in terms of factors that affect educational attainment and preparation for college, implies that college admissions staff need to be sensitive to the background characteristics of Hispanic college applicants when interpreting Hispanic candidates' college admissions data. This sensitivity should go beyond knowledge of Hispanic applicants' ethnic subidentity to include an understanding of factors that Hispanic applicants must overcome in preparing for college. A further implication is that college administration and other staff need to use information on Hispanics' background to create effective services for Hispanic students in all areas of their university experiences.

Attention will now be turned to a brief survey of issues not covered in depth in this report that need to be considered in a more intensive study of factors affecting Hispanic students' college achievement and its prediction.

OTHER FACTORS INFLUENCING HISPANIC STUDENTS' COLLEGE ACHIEVEMENT

At present, the empirical research literature on Hispanics' higher educational achievement in college, which is not focused on prediction of college grades, is hard to identify, scattered in terms of its institutional origin, and not well organized according to issues for investigation. With the exception of a recent study by Astin and Burciaga (1981), research at a national survey level has not been undertaken. One reason for this state of affairs is to be expected. Just as with predictive validity studies, most research studies of Hispanics' college achievement and student characteristics are based on study of single institutions. A second reason for lack of coherence in research in the area is the immense span of relevant issues that might be addressed. With the principal exception of the Astin and Burciaga (1981) and Vasquez (1978) studies that will be mentioned, the current review does not survey the sparse empirical research literature on Hispanics' college achievement unrelated to prediction of grades or the more plentiful body of expository papers on factors underlying Hispanics' failure to attain and complete college. The reason for not considering these sources of information is due to the more focused purpose of this report and to the lack of resources to pursue such an endeavor. Nonetheless, recurrent conjectures put forth in the literature and findings from selected research studies are here cited for possible systematic research on the topic of this report.[11]

Payán et al. (1982) list a number of factors affecting Hispanics' education in terms of two broad categories: "personal factors" and "institutional factors." While the Payán et al. list is not intended as a theoretical base for research studies, it helps identify issues in need of investigation. Under the category "personal factors" fall such student characteristics as:

- gender of student;

- educational and vocational aspirations;

- major field of study choice;

- academic self-concept and self-confidence;

- study habits, including adjustment to college routines;

- social and emotional adjustment at college.

To the foregoing personal factors we might also add on the basis of the present report:

- proficiency in Spanish and English;

- academic preparation for college work;

- students' financial needs and personal needs related to family responsibilities;

- personal characteristics arising from migration-immigration experiences of students;

- students' general acculturation to U.S. life and the social value systems of students;

- age and maturity of students.

Under the category "institutional factors," Payán et al. (1982) list:

- structural characteristics of the college or university: type of control (e.g., public, independent, Catholic); level of degrees offered; size; location (including cultural setting and proximity to Hispanic population); gender composition of student body; characteristic instructional approaches; general missions; traditions (including reputed academic standards);

- general institutional commitment to the education of Hispanics;

- ethnic composition of faculty (by department) and staff;

- faculty-student interaction; perceptions of the nature and quality of characteristic interactions between students and, in particular, Anglo professors; faculty seen as accepting and supportive; presence of (Hispanic faculty) role models;

- peer support systems: presence of/student use of peer counseling, tutoring, and other services;

- institution-operated student support services: presence of/student participation in special orientation programs, advisory services, remedial/tutorial opportunities, and extracurricular activities for Hispanic students;

- housing: in particular, characteristic academic attitudes of other residents;

- financial aid: type, amount, information about, accorded to the student; and

- "sponsorship": existence of an organization, internal or external to the campus (e.g., a corporate, religious, or scholarship granting body), that has taken a personal interest in the student's academic career.

The foregoing span of issues is relevant at two principal points related to the objectives of the present report. First, there is a need to understand how factors such as the foregoing affect Hispanic students' preparation and candidacy for college. Second, there is a need to understand how factors such as the foregoing go on to affect Hispanic students' college achievement and college experiences. While some studies reviewed in this report have touched on the issues mentioned, the very span of the issues listed and the variation of background among

Hispanics suggest that much information useful to improving higher educational opportunities for Hispanics remains to be discovered.

Two recent studies on one group of Hispanics — Chicanos — by Astin and Burciaga (1981) and by Vasquez (1978) identify new directions for needed research on Hispanics' college access and college attainment. Brief highlights from both studies help suggest issues for further research.

The Astin and Burciaga (1981) study, "Chicanos in Higher Education: Progress and Attainment," included discussion of a national survey study conducted by the Higher Education Research Institute under funding of a larger minority higher education study by the Ford Foundation (Astin, 1982). One major source of data in the report was the Cooperative Institutional Research Program. The findings of the Astin and Burciaga study are not reviewed in detail here since the study was not available until late in the development of the present report. A critique of the broader study on which it is based is found in *La Red* (1982). There are two principal benefits to be derived from the study in the present context. First, the study conveys the importance of national longitudinal and nomothetic survey research on Hispanics' candidacy and access to college; college achievement and college experience patterns; development of career plans; and completion of college training. Second, the study sets forth some findings that help identify alternative variables that might be used to predict Hispanics' college potential and college success.

In the area of predictor measures of college success, Astin and Burciaga concluded that high school grades were the best predictors of Chicano college success. They qualified this conclusion in terms of further findings that showed that persistence in school, expectations about schooling success, and background measures of parental education and socioeconomic status were also meaningfully related to predictions of Chicanos' grades during the first two years of college and also to prediction of Hispanics' successful completion of college. Astin and Burciaga further concluded:

> Chicano students who scored high on the verbal subtest of the Scholastic Aptitude Test (SAT) tended to make good grades in college, even after their high school grades were taken into account. Thus, language proficiency seems especially important to the college performance of Chicanos. (Astin and Burciaga, 1981, p. 631)

It should be noted that the Astin and Burciaga report of their study provides only limited data supporting the foregoing points that have been raised. There is a need for independent replication of the findings and for more detailed reporting of the corresponding data analyses. The issue regarding the relationship of Hispanics' verbal admissions subtest scores to college grades needs more careful specification and clarification. When considered in the light of the present report, the Astin and Burciaga finding suggests two complementary but contrasting hypotheses. First, there is a need to investigate how Hispanic college candidates' proficiency in English moderates candidates' college admissions test scores and other measures of academic preparation for college. The Astin and Burciaga conclusion that Hispanics' college admissions verbal test scores added to prediction of Hispanics' college grades — beyond the level of prediction obtained from knowledge of high school grades — applied only for verbal admissions test scores in the higher range of scores for Hispanics. This result supports the value of verbal admissions test scores for some Hispanics. A second complementary but contrasting hypothesis suggests that verbal college admissions test scores are less useful in predicting Hispanics' college grades — beyond information given by high school grades — when Hispanics score lower on the verbal component of college admissions tests. The research challenge thus raised is to investigate more carefully and in more detail how the predictive validity of Hispanics' admissions test score data (in the context of other admissions data) is affected by Hispanics' familiarity with English and with the variety of English used on admissions tests. Of course, a related issue on the criterion side of prediction is how Hispanics' familiarity with the academic variety of English used at school and in college affects academic performance.

The Astin and Burciaga study also found that Chicanos' college grades during the first two years of college were related to age of students and parental income level. Older Chicano students and Chicano students from families with higher income tended to obtain higher college grades during the first two years of college. The results of the regression analyses leading to the foregoing conclusion were not described in detail in the Astin and Burciaga (1981) report, and thus there remains room for more detailed interpretation of these results.

Astin and Burciaga found that three college environmental variables contributed to prediction of Chicanos' college grades during the first two years of college. Chicanos who enrolled in private colleges tended to earn lower grades than Chicanos enrolled in nonprivate colleges. A second finding was that attendance at an institution with a high proportion of women was positively related to Chicanos' college grades. Lastly, it was found that Chicanos who lived on campus tended to earn higher college grades than Chicanos who lived off campus. The statistical analyses supporting the foregoing conclusions were not presented in detail in the Astin and Burciaga (1981) report.

College environmental variables in themselves are not predictor variables of college achievement in the same sense as measures collected prior to college admission. College environmental variables are concurrent predictors of college success. However, it is the case that some criterion measures of college achievement, such as graduation, might be predicted in advance by college environmental variables. In this sense, college institution factors may function as predictors of college performance in advance of performance.

Besides college persistence, grade-point average, and college graduation status, the Astin and Burciaga study relied on one other measure to investigate Chicano students' adjustment to college. This measure was an index of students' satisfaction with college. The satisfaction index reflected students' responses to questionnaire items pertaining to involvement in college programs and satisfaction with services and activities at college. While the satisfaction index covered many dimensions of college experience, it turned out that Chicanos' satisfaction with their mathematics preparation for college was the student input variable that was most strongly associated with college satisfaction. Astin and Burciaga (1981, p. 64) commented that such a finding might be interpreted to reflect the importance of Chicano students' judgment of their academic worth as an indicator of their adjustment to college. The study also found that Chicano students' satisfaction with college was positively related to parental income, freshman expectations regarding ultimate success in college, and preference for a major in the arts and humanities versus a major in the social sciences.

Chicano students who attended private versus nonprivate college institutions were found to be less satisfied with college than other Chicanos, and it is noteworthy that this finding occurred coupled with the finding that Chicanos earned lower grades in the first two years of college if they attended private rather than nonprivate colleges. Interestingly, Chicanos who lived on campus tended to be more dissatisfied than Chicanos who lived off campus. According to Astin and Burciaga, this result contrasts with the general finding that living on campus has positive effects on students overall.

The Astin and Burciaga research study included a longitudinal investigation of 315 Chicanos who entered college as freshmen in 1971 expecting a bachelor's degree and who were questionnaire respondents in 1980. Among this group of Chicanos, attainment of a bachelor's degree was related to good grades in high school and to high self-ratings of writing ability when students were freshmen. No mention is made of the association of admissions test scores with baccalaureate attainment. According to Astin and Burciaga, the finding that freshman self-judgments of writing skills were positive predictors of attainment of a bachelor's degree supports the importance of language proficiency skills in Chicanos' college attainment. College grades among Chicanos making up the 1971–80 longitudinal sample were positively related to high school grades, parental socioeconomic background, and nonprivate college attendance. These results from the longitudinal sample of Chicanos were thus the same as results reported for Chicano college students in the study at large who were not part of a longitudinal sample.

Other data from an extended 1971–80 sample of Chicanos used to augment the basic 1971–80 longitudinal sample indicated that certain institutional factors had long-term effects on Chicanos' educational attainment. To quote Astin and Burciaga (1981, p. 70):

> Attendance at a high-quality institution (as measured by the prestige, selectivity, tuition, per-student expenditures for educational purposes, and average faculty salary) substantially increases the Chicano student's chances of completing the baccalaureate and of pursuing advanced training.

Among the range of topics covered in the Astin and Burciaga work are the career development patterns, graduate school experiences, and professional academic experiences of Chicanos who formed the 1971–80 longitudinal samples. While the results of this part of the report are not discussed in detail here, it is noteworthy to mention that Chicano students' perceptions of their academic worth and adjustment to college were positively related to achievement criteria such as completion of a bachelor's degree, completion of graduate school, and development of professional status as academicians. Findings of the report also suggested that Chicanos pursuing a higher education or professional academic status also perceived that their social values and beliefs about social equity contrasted considerably with those of nonminority college staff.

Before concluding the present section and synthesizing directions for further research, it will be useful to mention a study by Vasquez (1978). This study dealt with the college experiences of Chicana and Anglo women at a large southwestern university. Citation of this study in the present context is important not only because of its focus on the issue of gender, but also because it dramatizes how expansion of the scope of college predictive validity studies—beyond concern for prediction of college grades from high school grades and admissions test scores—to include concern for influences of background and personal variables deepens our understanding of factors affecting prediction of Hispanics' success in college. The Vasquez study investigated the association between Chicana and Anglo female students' college grades and ability to persist in college with the following classes of variables: students' background characteristics; high school grades; students' financial situation and source of income; personal income; student aspirations and expectations about grades and graduation; students' family motivational climate; students' age; students' ethnicity; students' scores on a college environmental stress index; and students' bicultural orientation (Chicanos only).

The results of the Vasquez study suggested that college grades and persistence in college were not predictable in quite the same way for Anglo and Chicana women. High versus low college grade-point average for Anglo women was best predicted from high school grade-point average, students' judgments of "importance of maintaining a 'B' average in college" and self-prediction of "chances of graduating from college." In the case of Chicanos, the results showed that high versus low grade-point average was best predicted by students' high school grades and "mother's encouragement to do well in school." Persistence versus nonpersistence in college attendance for Anglo women was best predicted by students' "self-prediction of chances of graduation from college," "importance of maintaining a 'B' average," and "importance of graduation to father." Persistence of Chicana women was not very well predicted by any variables used as predictors. Vasquez indicated that Chicana women who had low GPA and who were unable to remain in college had nearly as high academic expectations of themselves as Chicana and Anglo women who received good grades and remained in college. Thus, whereas expectations of academic achievement worked well as predictors of Anglo women's persistence in college, these same expectations did not predict Chicana women's persistence in college. Some evidence in the Vasquez research further suggested that Chicana women may need to compensate more than Anglo women in development of their academic expectations and academic self-esteem. Anglo women were more likely than Chicana women to come from home environments where family members expressed high hopes about the academic and educational attainment of their female children.

The kind of results mentioned from the Vasquez study indicates that much may be gained by more closely investigating background and personal variables mitigating prediction of Hispanic college students' achievement. The issues of gender-related factors affecting educational attainment and achievement addressed in the Vasquez work are extremely important in the case of Hispanics, because of Hispanic cultural influences on the development of Hispanic women's self-identity and academic aspirations.

The purpose of the foregoing discussions of the work of Astin and Burciaga (1981) and of Vasquez (1978) has been to stimulate the breadth of inquiry that is possible in studies of factors affecting prediction of Hispanic students' college achievement. It is readily appreciated that the expanse of issues that might be investigated is quite immense and subject to many different forms of coherent inquiry on both theoretical and practical grounds. In addition to more accurate theoretical models on which to base research, careful attention will need to be paid to adequate frameworks for data analysis and for detailed descriptions of results. The next section of this chapter outlines broad directions for structuring a productive program of research on prediction of Hispanics' college achievement. The final section of the report gives specific attention to some examples of research studies that might prove highly useful from the perspective of a college admissions testing program.

DIRECTIONS FOR RESEARCH

The need for research on prediction of Hispanics' achievement in college does not occur in a vacuum removed from real educational policy issues. While research on Hispanics as a population may contribute to social science and education as fields of knowledge, there are fundamental educational equity policy issues that mandate practical concern for research on Hispanics' higher education attainment. From an educational equity perspective, at least three issues stand out:

- The first issue concerns academic, social, and personal preparation of Hispanics for college and the degree to which Hispanics benefit from the U.S. education system enroute to college candidacy.

- The second issue concerns the actual process by which Hispanics become college candidates, the profiles presented by Hispanic students as college candidates, and the selection processes enacted in admission of Hispanics to college.

- The third issue concerns what happens to Hispanics after they enter college and whether or not admission to college and college experiences lead to acceptable academic achievement, graduation, and other benefits of a college education.

From an equity perspective, each of the issues cited — preparation for college, college admission, college experience — is associated with many basic and important questions regarding improvement of Hispanics' access to higher education and prediction of Hispanics' higher education achievement. Given that the orientation of the present report is towards improving prediction of Hispanics' higher education achievement, each of the three issues mentioned generates many questions for research from the perspective of college admissions testing programs. In addition, other research topics cut across issues or are outside of the issues but are nonetheless essential to studies of prediction of Hispanics' college achievement. The list of organizing questions for research that is offered here is intended to be more suggestive than comprehensive.

Research on the Precollege Preparation, Aspirations, and Background of Hispanic College Candidates

Much of the empirical evidence cited in this report suggests that U.S. Hispanic high school students are not receiving the same quality of precollege education as nonminority U.S. students. A fundamental question in need of research from a college admissions testing program orientation is: How can there be more accurate assessment of the academic and educationally relevant skills of Hispanic college candidates? Ability to benefit from college and to learn in college implies in part a concept of "potentiality." In the case of Hispanics and other minority students, the notion of collegiate academic ability should include not only the assessed academic ability of students but also the academic growth potential of students. Restated, the question that has been raised is how to recognize the positive, adaptive characteristics of Hispanic college candidates in the face of their profile as candidates. In many cases, the college admissions test scores and high school academic records of Hispanics may not be commensurate with students' potential ability to succeed in college. Research on the part of college admissions testing programs needs to undertake a more thorough and comprehensive analysis of Hispanics' preparation for college and of personal and background factors that may moderate prediction of success in college. Research in this area ought to be undertaken at points in time preceding Hispanic high school students' formal college candidacy, as well as afterwards. Discussion of the latter approach is deferred until treatment of needed college admissions research.

Prior to becoming college candidates, Hispanic high school students are subject to school, home, and community experiences that profoundly affect chances for college candidacy. Within the high school context preceding application for college, we need to understand how the college aspirations of Hispanic students are determined and what academic, counseling and high school institutional factors affect the chances that Hispanics will decide to apply for college. A related question is what factors affect Hispanics' choice of college institutions. Outside of the school, factors such as the economic needs of students' families, the expectation of parents about their children's education, and the sociocultural influence of students' communities and peer networks affect Hispanics' decision and choices for college candidacy. The sociocultural background of Hispanics, including value orientation and language background, also exerts influence on students' decision to plan for college candidacy. Research is needed accordingly in these latter areas.

Both national large sample and case study research are needed on the foregoing issues. Broad survey research on the characteristics of Hispanic students, and their language and cultural background factors affecting higher education aspirations before college application, would be informative to high school counseling staff and college admissions staff on the kinds of influences that affect Hispanic students' preparation and aspirations for college. The practical importance of such work will lie in the conversion of research findings into information that high school staff could use to help Hispanic students prepare for college and develop aspirations for college candidacy. Publication and dissemination of survey research findings on Hispanic high school students thus need to be planned carefully in order for such research to have practical value.

Case study research on Hispanic students' development of college aspirations, such as the work presently proposed by Payán et al. (1982), and research on Hispanic students' academic development are also needed. Case study research based on an intensive survey of Hispanic students at a few high school institutions is valuable to suggest because it may be more sensitive than a survey regarding the interaction of different kinds of variables that affect students' aspirations and plans for a college education. Case study methods may derive detailed information on this topic through the conduct of intensive personal interviews with Hispanic students, Hispanic families, and high school staff.

Two additional areas for case study research that seem promising are the process by which Hispanic students decide to take college admissions tests and how Hispanic high school students' aspirations for college are affected by knowledge of their college admissions tests scores. The decision to take a college admissions test is a benchmark decision; it represents a step that positively or negatively constrains high school students' future options for college candidacy. Almost as important as the decision to take a test is the decision of which admissions test to take. Some institutions require the ACT test while others require the SAT test. Thus, students who take the ACT test or the SAT test make unintended, as well as deliberate, decisions about what colleges they may consider application for. The constraining implications of what admissions test to take, if any, thus is an important issue affecting what colleges Hispanic students may aspire to apply to for admission.

Once a student takes an admissions test, a further issue is how results from a test affect Hispanic high school students' college aspirations and high school academic preparation. Since it is a fact that Hispanic students on the average score lower than nonminority students on college admissions tests, it is natural to inquire about what effect test scores have on Hispanic students' college aspirations. For example, one question is whether lower-than-average test scores have more of an effect of depressing Hispanics' college aspirations than is the case for nonminority high school students. Case study research is needed on the foregoing questions in order to guide formulation of national survey research that could prove more widely informative to high school staff, college admissions staff, and college admissions testing programs on the impact of test scores on Hispanic students' college aspirations.

Case study research also may have value for the high school institutions studied. If there is adequate planning, the results of case studies may be used by students, families, and high school staff in improving Hispanic students' motivation and preparation for college.

A third role for research in investigation of Hispanic high school students' development of aspirations and skills for college is in planning and evaluation of intervention programs targeted at high schools with high representation of Hispanic students. The College Board project "Options for Excellence," based in San Antonio, Texas, and funded with a grant from the Minnie Stevens Piper Foundation, represents an example of an intervention program, involving many Mexican American students, that could draw on research in optimizing its outcomes. In the San Antonio project, an extensive programmatic effort is being made to improve students' knowledge of their academic skills, their exposure to course work related to college, and their interaction with college recruiters. The conduct of the San Antonio project merits evaluation in terms of its procedures and outcomes. One important role of research in such a program could be to contribute to objective documentation of the effectiveness of the program. The findings of research on an intervention program may be of further value since they can serve as a prima facie resource for assisting future programmatic intervention with high school students who are primarily Hispanic. While the San Antonio project has been cited here, research may be seen to have a similar value in the evaluation, or else planning, of other programmatic interventions to improve Hispanic high school students' preparation and access to college.

Research on the Process of Hispanic College Admissions

Research in the present area concerns the admissions process and its outcome once Hispanics formally have applied for college admission. Conduct of research may involve large sample methodology or case study methodology.

The resources of national college admissions testing programs are invaluable in addressing large sample research questions arising in this area. Within their student candidate data bases, testing programs have information not only on students' education and familial background, aspirations, college curriculum interests, and test scores, they also have information on students' choice of colleges to have their test scores sent to. In the case of Hispanics, it is thus possible to make a nationally-based inquiry about the candidate profiles of Hispanics aspiring to attend colleges that invite admissions test scores of candidates. Analysis of this Hispanic data would help us understand the academic and background characteristics of Hispanics taking college admissions tests and the college aspirations of these Hispanic candidates. The language background research reviewed in this report suggests that language proficiency items on existing admissions test candidate questionnaires should be augmented in order to improve their usefulness. In the final section of the report, this specific issue is addressed and an example is offered of concrete research that might be carried out.

Conduct of research summarizing the profile characteristics of Hispanic college candidates from admissions testing program data ought not to be a sporadic or one-time endeavor. There is considerable value in periodically updating Hispanic candidate profiles; such updated profiles would be useful in assessing change in the population of Hispanic admissions test takers. While yearly development of summaries seems ideal, summaries might be pursued at less frequent intervals, such as once every two to three years.

Institutionally-based survey research might be enacted to investigate differences in the profiles of Hispanic college candidates who successfully gain admission to an institution versus the profiles of those who do not. A survey orientation would be appropriate for institutions with high numbers of Hispanic candidates for admission. At institutions with a low number of Hispanic applicants, case study research might be more appropriate as a means for learning how Hispanic applicants fare in the admissions process.

Regardless of whether a survey or case study approach is taken, one of the most important questions in need of investigation from the viewpoint of admissions testing programs is the role played by admissions test scores in admissions decisions. Among many Hispanics, there is a strong belief that admissions test scores are often used as a deciding criterion in college admissions. There is also a prevalent belief that institutions generally use cutoff scores on admissions tests in rejecting applicants. Of course, use of cutoff scores is discouraged by admissions testing programs. Information is needed on how college institutions actually use Hispanic candidates' test score data. The value of research on this topic would be to assist testing programs in developing more articulated guidelines for colleges on appropriate uses of test scores and the consequences of misuse. Articulation of guidelines for test score use are needed since institutions will vary in terms of their institutional characteristics, academic emphasis, and student admissions policies.

Case study research of how particular institutions or systems of institutions enact the admissions process would seem particularly valuable. There is a need for a more in-depth understanding of how different styles and systems for making admissions decisions at institutions affect Hispanic candidates' chances for admission. For example, there is a need to understand better the interpersonal and decision-making dynamics of admissions procedures that involve participation of Hispanic and other minority-background admissions staff. A question here is whether or not the active participation of Hispanic admission staff improves the acceptance rates of Hispanics and other minorities to a college.

Regarding the topic of prediction of Hispanics' college achievement, case study research on the admissions process might be capable of carefully documenting how academic capabilities of students are assessed and how prediction of success in college is substantiated by admissions staff. Followup research might investigate the accuracy of admissions staffs' prediction of students' success in college. Case studies of the admissions process could also lead to the identification of Hispanic student characteristics (e.g., high achievement motivation, interest in community affairs) that, if cultivated through college experience, might lead to accomplishments that would be indicators of college success. Such added criteria of college success might augment grades as a standard for achievement in college for Hispanics. Case studies of the admissions process could also thus show how candidate characteristics beyond admissions test scores and high school grades contribute to assessment of the college achievement potential of students. The problem of identifying suitable alternative criteria of college achievement is discussed later in this chapter.

One important area in need of survey and case study research is how the academic credentials and financial need characteristics of Hispanic college candidates are related to offers and packaging of financial aid and other services. One question that needs to be asked is how the financial aid and student services offered Hispanic students are affected by information on students' academic qualifications as well as by students' financial need. Explicitly needing attention is the extent to which financial aid staff are aware of the characteristics of Hispanic students and how awareness of student characteristics affects financial aid offers. Surveys of financial aid officers' knowledge of Hispanic college candidates and financial needs have been sponsored previously by the College Entrance Examination Board (Ferrin, Jonsen, and Trimble, 1972; and Payán, 1981). Such research is relevant and worthwhile for investigating the issues raised; however, there is a need for further studies to draw out information of a more fine-grained character on the impact of financial aid in Hispanics' college candidacy and college admissions. In addition, research is needed that investigates how institutional management of finance affects financial aid available to Hispanic college candidates (Olivas, 1981).

Attention is now turned to some research priorities concerned with understanding Hispanics' college experiences that are relevant to prediction of Hispanics' college achievement. As before, the perspective taken is to mention research that is of high relevance to an admissions testing program.

Research on Hispanics' Range of College Achievements and College Experiences

The extent of issues in need of investigation in the area to be discussed is quite immense, given the earlier discussions provided in this chapter and the report as a whole. The concern of this report with prediction of Hispanic students' college achievement makes it possible to synthesize two global categories of issues that organize topics for research investigation in the present area. The first global category of issues concerns what kind and range of accomplishments in college identify alternative concepts of college achievement. The second global category of issues pertains to what kind and range of college experiences serve as intervening moderator variables, or else as concurrent predictor variables of alternative forms of college achievement.

The question of how to conceptualize achievement in college is nontrivial. Existing predictive validity studies of college achievement have tended to rely on early college grades as indicators of college achievement. It is possible to conceptualize a range of college achievement indicators including and going beyond college grades. The following list suggests one way in which areas of achievement in college might be conceptualized:

- institutional success in producing Hispanic college graduates in particular academic areas;

- students' progress towards graduation, given institutional and academic program requirements;

- students' academic success as marked by grades, rank in class, other achievements in courses, development of academic breadth and depth, and development of particular academic skills;

- students' development of career and professional plans and plans for possible further schooling;

- students' development of social and personal values associated with both greater long-term societal adaptation and adaptation to college;

- students' nonacademic achievements arising out of college experience, such as public service accomplishments, contributions to artistic endeavors, etc.

The categorization of college achievement that has been mentioned above clearly goes beyond academic achievement as reflected in college grades. The concern of college admissions testing programs with early college grades as a criterion for the prediction of college success at the point of admission into college makes sense. Early college grades are useful in helping predict students' chances to succeed at college entry. Further grades are numerical measures and freshman college grades are earned in close proximity to admissions decisions. In predictive validity studies, it is a well known phenomenon that temporal closeness between prediction and criterion measures is typically an important factor in establishing validity of prediction. These qualities of early college grades make them useful as indicators of college achievement at the outset of college. Other criteria representing college achievement and college success are possible, particularly over the long-term span of college experience, and this fact is indeed acknowledged in the range of research studies sponsored by college admissions testing programs on college experiences. In the case of Hispanics, there is great value in widening the range of college achievement indicators that may reflect accomplishments students undertake in completing college. Not only is there a need for expanding the range of criteria for success in college as suggested above, there is also a need to explore within categories alternative ways in which achievement may be conceived.

Research is called into play as a method by which to establish and operationalize assessment of alternative criteria of college achievement. Research further may serve the purpose of establishing evidence of connections, dependency, and suitability among alternative measures of college achievement.

One important issue for research that will arise in establishing a broader range of criteria describing Hispanics' college achievement is whether the same criteria have the same meaning and validity for Hispanics as for non-Hispanics. Thus, for example, would it always be fair to believe that speed in completing college is the same indicator of Hispanics' achievement in college as is the case for non-minority students? The answer in this case is clearly "No," given the added pitfalls that Hispanics face in completing college.

Another important issue that arises in conceptualizing alternative measures of Hispanics' college achievement is the degree of personal, social, and academic growth that Hispanics must manifest in order to complete college. A recent report by the Commission on the Higher Education of Minorities (Higher Education Research Institute, 1982) forwards the notion of a value-added model of minorities' achievement in college. From a value-added approach, growth in minority students' capabilities to succeed in college represents a significant aspect of achievement in college. Many Hispanic and other minority students must endure more change and steeper growth in skills related to college adjustment and academic achievement than do nonminority students. Thus, in completing college successfully, many minority students have gained more from college than nonminority students. Since minority students' gains reflect personal effort on the part of students to attain gains, it may be argued that colleges need to recognize some aspects of minority students' gains not reflected in traditional college academic evaluations as additional bona fide achievements of minority students.

A contrastive analysis of various ways to characterize achievement of Hispanic college students needs to integrate and incorporate value-added and traditional notions of achievement together across the achievement areas that have been outlined. As mentioned earlier in conceptualizing different domains of college achievement, it will prove scientifically invaluable to empirically establish and compare different models for college achievement. A contrast in the utility of different models for representing Hispanics' college achievement is necessary as a step to better understand how to improve prediction of Hispanics' college achievement.

Case study and large sample study research on alternative criteria for Hispanics' college achievement are both needed. Case study research ought to precede large sample research in order to provide some concrete directions for large sample research. Case study research might involve in-depth interviews of Hispanic students to ascertain their history of accomplishments in college and the relationships of these accomplishments to their background and personal characteristics. Interview information could be coupled with the study of archival college records of students and with interviews with college staff. The motive behind case studies, carried out, for example, at a few institutional sites, would be to learn about key alternative indicators of college achievement that might be operationalized as questionnaire items on a subsequent large sample survey of Hispanic college students. The results of a large sample survey of Hispanics' college achievement and the relationship of achievement to other factors could be used in turn as the basis for creating predictive validity studies of Hispanics' achievement in college.

There is a logical point to clarifying what can be meant by Hispanics' achievement in college as a precursor to thinking about how to predict college achievement. The point is simply that we cannot understand the utility of predictor measures of college achievement unless we understand the characteristics of what we are trying to predict.

A second relevant point that has been raised here is that college grades are but one useful way in which to conceptualize achievement in college. In the case of Hispanics, and other students at large, alternative ways in which college achievement may be interpreted are invaluable in understanding students' educational attainment.

The suggestion that there is a need for research comparing and contrasting different notions of Hispanics' college achievement should not be taken as a proscription for research of a more limited and less ambitious nature. Clearly, there is ongoing value in studying prediction of a single criterion of college achievement, such as college grades.

Economy of scale, resources, and the immediate value of returns on research may constrain frequent pursuit of the more ambitious strategies described. Nonetheless, in the longer course of research, it is imperative to point out the fundamental and pressing need for research comparing the validity and utility of different notions of Hispanics' college achievement.

Attention is now turned towards categorizing student college experience and institutional variables that might serve as concurrent predictors or moderators of college achievement.

Based largely on the outline of Payán et al. (1982), the work of Nieves (1982), and other sources mentioned in this report, we may identify at least five overall dimensions of students' personal characteristics that can affect college achievement. These dimensions are:

- aspirations,

- academic skills and academic self-management,

- psychosocial adjustment,

- communicative skills,

- financial needs of students and familial financial demands on students.

Hispanic students' personal realization of the foregoing sorts of factors in college bears directly on students' ability to function and achieve in a college environment. Consistent with previous discussion, note that many of the personal characteristic dimensions listed themselves might serve as independent factors depicting college achievement. Research on the impact of these factors on academic achievement necessitates consideration of institutional characteristics that provide the nurturing environment for college achievement.

Again distilling from the outline provided by Payán et al. (1982) and other sources in this report, we may synthesize at least six major dimensions of college institutions that affect Hispanic students' success in college. These college dimensions are:

- structural and administrative characteristics;

- academic characteristics;

- student services, financial aid programs, and student activities;

- presence of minority students, minority faculty, and minority staff in a college;

- prominent social and cultural values of college students, faculty, and college staff;

- community environment surrounding a college, including socioeconomic, sociocultural, and racial integration of a community.

In investigating how Hispanic students' college experience affects college achievement, it is necessary to trace the interaction of students' personal characteristics with institutional factors. For different domains of college achievement, it would be valuable to investigate how achievement behaviors in a given domain are influenced by personal and institutional characteristics. To the extent that Hispanic students are different from nonminority students, Hispanic students' ability to achieve will be marked by some college experiences that will differ in their presence and significance from nonminority students' experiences in college. Some of the differences in college experiences between Hispanics and nonminority students will lead to differences in patterns of college achievement. It may also be possible that some differences in college experiences between Hispanics and non-Hispanics will not be associated with factors creating differences in college achievement across the two groups.

Research in the area of Hispanics' college experiences and their effect on college achievement is extremely important from an admissions testing program perspective. The findings of such research can help clarify what aspects of college achievement are amenable to prediction on the basis of candidate information prior to college admission. Research in the area will help determine the benefits and limits of college admissions test scores, high school grades, and other admissions measures as predictors of college achievement. For example, in the case of college admissions tests, at present there exist contradictory and diverse views on the value of tests as predictors of Hispanics' college achievement. Among the major criticisms are that test scores do not predict college grades well and that some of Hispanics' accomplishments in college are not represented by grades. Another criticism is that the college environment and its hospitality to Hispanic students and not test scores are the critical factors in predicting achievement of Hispanic college students. Research of the sort that is advised in this report would help create a more realistic and articulated understanding of different forms of Hispanic college achievement and how achievement might be predicted from admissions information.

As with research on Hispanic high school students' precollege experiences, research on college achievement and college experiences would benefit from both case study and large sample research methodologies. The uniqueness of many institutional characteristics and variation of the hospitability of institutions to Hispanics provide grounds for suggesting that investigation of Hispanics' success in college ought to stress how students can perform in particular college environments given their background, personal characteristics, and academic characteristics.

Survey and case study research on the background and institutional experiences of Hispanic students at similar college institutions should be conducted. Questionnaire and interview research could be conducted simultaneously at several college institutions that share similar institutional and geographic characteristics. By concentrating on a similar group of campuses, it would be possible to learn how Hispanic students are accommodating to similar environmental factors and how students' personal characteristics interact with institutional characteristics to affect college achievement. Questionnaire and interview content could address the sociocultural, language, and academic backgrounds of students—including how these factors were realized at the point of college admission—in order to investigate how the profile of Hispanic college candidates is related to college experiences and college achievement. Under the best of all circumstances, archival admissions record information might be used in studies of the sort described in order to increase the reliability and validity of measures.

Special Topics for Research

In some way or another, all of the directions for research that have thus far been listed have pertained to broadly conceived issues relevant to predicting Hispanics' college achievement. The present section will briefly discuss a few specific topic areas for research that could stand alone or else be made a part of needed research of the sort that has thus far been described. The example study areas suggested are as follows:

- language proficiency in English, and language background of Hispanic college candidates. The role of language factors in moderating prediction of Hispanics' college achievement;

- influence of choice of major, and academic evaluation standards on prediction of Hispanics' college achievement;

- effects of academic intervention, self-management improvement intervention and counseling on college admissions test performance, academic skills development, and college achievement of Hispanics;

- improved statistical models for the prediction of Hispanics' college achievement from candidate information.

Language proficiency and language background. As has been brought out throughout this report, the influence of language proficiency and background factors on prediction of Hispanics' college achievement is a very important and practical area for research. From an admissions testing program point of view, such research is critical because both admissions test performance and behavior in college may be affected by Hispanics' familiarity with English and communicative skills in English. Based on the research reviewed in this report, there is emerging evidence that variation in Hispanic students' English proficiency and language background may affect prediction of college achievement.

A specific project or series of studies that would be useful in improving prediction of Hispanics' college achievement in light of language proficiency and language background could be founded on an augmentation of testing programs' college candidate questionnaire items. Candidate questionnaires administered to testing registrants could be modified to include more language background and language proficiency items. For example, new items could be added that address candidates' history of educational exposure to English and a non-English language. Of course, the term "non-English" would refer to Spanish in the case of almost all Hispanics, but it would be important from an admissions testing program perspective to create new language items on candidate questionnaires that would lead to potentially valuable language and educational information on candidates from other ethnolinguistic groups.

The presence of a variety of socioeconomic, academic, and aspiration items on testing programs' college candidate questionnaires could permit a statistical investigation of how strongly related candidates' academic credentials, high school grades, and college admissions test scores are to language background and language proficiency factors. The results of investigating connections between Hispanics' language characteristics and college candidate credentials would be useful to higher educational institutions in the admissions process. In evaluating the credentials of Hispanic candidates, colleges could take into account how language background of students might affect the interpretation of candidate information. Hispanic students who demonstrated an intensive exposure to Spanish, coupled with limited English exposure outside school, might be students whose admissions test scores and high school grades could be less reliable predictors of college grades than would be the case for other students. Information of this sort could trigger admissions staff to be more careful and qualitatively sensitive in evaluating the college potential of Hispanic students from the language background described.

Choice of major and academic evaluation standards. Research is needed on the academic preferences of Hispanic college students and on how enrollment in different courses is related to Hispanics' admissions profiles. In order to predict Hispanics' success in college, we need to investigate the match or mismatch between the coursework that Hispanics undertake in college and the academic background of Hispanics. Related to this issue are the course evaluation standards that Hispanics may encounter in different areas of college course work. Some of the lack of relationship between Hispanics' high school grades and admissions test scores with college grades could be due to course selection patterns and course evaluation patterns that Hispanics realize in college. Research in this area will help clarify how important Hispanic student language background, sociocultural background, and personal characteristics affect college achievement, taking into consideration the course work preferences of Hispanics.

Effects of intervention to improve Hispanics' academic and test performance. One of the most important areas for future research recently advocated in a major report by the Commission on the Higher Education of Minorities (Higher Education Research Institute, 1982) was on the effects of interventions designed to improve minorities' abilities to survive and succeed in college. A great range of research on this topic is needed on behalf of Hispanic students at both the precollege and college level. For example, the research needed might include: studies of precollege training programs to improve Hispanics' academic skills and college admissions test scores, and evaluation studies of precollege or college programs to improve Hispanics' self-control and study habits in an academic environment. In the case of the latter concern, for purposes of research, the preliminary work of Nieves (Office of Minority Education, Educational Testing Service, 1982) appears to be a promising framework within which to study the effects of a comprehensive program to train minority college students (and even minority high school students) in self-help and self-management techniques related to college survival. "Options for Excellence," which was mentioned earlier, represents an example of how an admissions testing program may pursue inquiry into this area.

Improved statistical models for predictive validity studies. Ongoing research is needed on formal models of a statistical nature that might be used in improving the prediction of college achievement of Hispanics and other minorities or women. A central concern is how college admissions staff might improve their procedures for predicting success in college. One of the most important issues to be faced is how to weigh those characteristics of Hispanic students that are not represented by high school grades and admissions test scores into admissions decisions. The issue is not to eliminate use of high school grades or test scores in admissions, but rather to have admissions decisions become more sensitive to the fuller range of positive characteristics that Hispanic college candidates possess that would predict success in college. As an example of the kind of research needed, Cardoza (1982) has recently begun development of a decision theory framework for admissions decisions involving Hispanic or other minority college candidates. The Cardoza work is interesting because it suggests that admissions staff might assign evaluations to information beyond high school grades and college admissions test scores in making admissions decisions. In the Cardoza work, the weights or utilities assigned to candidate characteristics are determined by a decision theory model that maximizes the expected utility or value of admissions decisions relative to an explicit admissions policy set forth by an institution. Within a framework such as that being explored by Cardoza, it may prove possible for college institutions to formally and quantitatively take into account some of Hispanic candidates' language and background characteristics that would mediate prediction of college success. While no practical admissions procedure is perfect in the sense of accepting all students who would succeed in college, a more explicit account of admissions decision making would allow the degree of error in admissions to be made more public and subject to democratic evaluation.

CLOSING COMMENTS

This report has ended with a lengthy discussion of needed research in improvement of the prediction of Hispanics' college success. The report as a whole has spanned a far-reaching universe of issues related to Hispanics' population characteristics and Hispanics' educational welfare in the United States. No attempt such as the present one should be considered comprehensive. The interconnection among issues and the reality that all relevant evidence could not be weighted in a single report such as this one implies that there will be gaps in the account rendered.

Indeed, we presently lack an adequate theoretical framework for minorities' education in the United States that would bind together all the requisite issues.

One of the major questions covered in this report is what role research might play in the improved prediction of Hispanics' higher education, relative to the practical everyday needs and practices of education institutions and admissions testing programs. This question has not been fully answered. Other policy issues are involved in deciding how to use educational resources and whether it is better to pay for programmatic research or else to invest resources in improving the immediate services available to students and college candidates. While we cannot expect a simple answer to this question of allocation of resources, there does seem to be a strong sentiment for using educational resources as efficiently as possible. One way in which research of the sort advocated in this report might be more efficient is to link its conduct and outcome to specific constituencies that might directly and immediately benefit from research findings. The resolution of how to allocate resources for research on improvement of prediction of Hispanics' college success will require a determined effort in order to have research directions and research findings accumulate in a coherent way that is productive to college admissions practices and educational practices in high school and college.

As a final comment, it should be recognized that a good number of the educational problems related to higher education access and achievement faced by Hispanics in the United States cannot be understood by isolated study of Hispanics apart from other segments of the population. While the present report has not presented analyses of higher education issues and problems affecting blacks, other minority groups, and students from low socioeconomic backgrounds in general, it seems evident that a more total and comprehensive treatment of issues needs to evolve from a concern for other groups in addition to Hispanics. It is hoped that the present report may provide input for this more ambitious and needed endeavor.

Appendix: Testing of Hispanics' Cognitive Skills

The survey orientation of the present report does not permit an extensive and thorough discussion of previous research on the validity of cognitive testing of Hispanics. For recent reviews and discussions of issues, the reader is referred to Padilla (1979), Aguirre (1980), Olmedo (1979), Laosa (1977), DeBlassie (1980), and Zirkel (1975). The following summary of issues is adapted from Padilla (1979) and Durán (1981, pp. 311–336); this discussion excludes specific studies of Hispanic college admissions test performance since those studies are reviewed in Chapters 4 and 5.

Early research on U.S. Hispanics' test performance has led to findings demonstrating that Hispanics score higher on "performance" (i.e., nonverbal) tests of general intelligence than on verbal general intelligence tests (for example, see Garth, Elson, and Morton, 1936; Shotwell, 1945; Cook and Arthur, 1951; Darcy, 1952). Research investigating whether Hispanics performed better on Spanish-version intelligence and achievement tests than on English-version counterparts has led to mixed findings. Some early studies (e.g., Mitchell, 1937; Mahakian, 1939) have shown that Hispanics perform better on Spanish-version than on English-version tests. However, other studies have shown no difference (e.g., Palmer and Gaffney, 1972) or have shown that Hispanics perform better on English-version than on Spanish-version tests (e.g., Keston and Jimenez, 1954). Each of these three patterns of findings is no doubt thoroughly confounded by the investigators' failure to establish the proficiency level of examinees in the vernacular or variety of Spanish and English used on tests. For example, in the Keston and Jimenez (1954) study, the Spanish version of Form L of the 1937 Stanford-Binet Intelligence Test administered to the children in the study was translated from English into Spanish by a professor at the National Institute of Psychotechniques, in Madrid. It seems highly unlikely that the vernacular of Spanish used on the translated tests corresponded very well to the norms for Spanish usage most familiar to the New Mexico children studied. Hence, without the prior assessment of children's proficiency in each of the languages of testing, there could be no way of averting the plausible conclusion that children's deficit performance in Spanish as compared to English reflected their degree of familiarity with the language variety used on tests.

The role language ability plays in Hispanics' mental test performance in Spanish and English has on occasion been more explicitly analyzed. For example, in two early papers Sanchez (1932, 1934) argued that vocabulary items on Spanish or English intelligence tests often do not reflect at all the normative language experiences of Hispanic children. Sanchez also argued that simple direct translation of English-version tests into Spanish was not necessarily an acceptable solution to the problem of improving control over the effects of vocabulary familiarity in testing. Development of translated forms of mental abilities tests mandates study of the difficulty of translated items for a population of examinees, as well as investigation, in general, of the reliability and validity of the newly translated test forms. In closing his 1934 paper, Sanchez pointed out the critical importance of assessing reading comprehension ability of Hispanics if one wishes to sensitively evaluate level of cognitive test performance and its dependence on language factors for written tests. It would seem that such a program of research would inevitably require comparison of the structure of written English likely to occur on tests with comparison of the structure or variety of English that Hispanic students show maximum skill in using. Such an enterprise would go beyond mere concern with vocabulary familiarity to encompass syntactic, idiomatic, and discourse structures that are likely to occur on tests in relation to Hispanics' knowledge of English. Concern would also have to be given to Hispanics' knowledge of Spanish as a source of strategies to deal with structures that occur in English.

As the following review of research studies indicates, there has been little sophisticated research on Hispanics' test performance from a linguistic or sociolinguistic standpoint.

Empirical research that specifically addressed how Hispanics' cognitive test performance is allied with language factors has shown that some young Hispanic children almost exclusively prefer the use of Spanish rather than English during administration of a general intelligence performance test (Anastasi and de Jesus, 1953). Other researchers have found that some Hispanic children's performance on general intelligence tests in English is constrained by English verbal comprehension skills and by ability to transfer English verbal skills to new situations (Christiansen and Livermore, 1970). In discussing a study by Killian (1971), Padilla (1979) cited the study as showing that bilingualism in a group of Spanish American children was allied with low WISC intelligence test scores relative to the higher WISC scores manifested by a group of monolingual-English Hispanic children, and the still higher WISC scores of a group of non-Hispanic monolingual-English children. In his summary, Padilla (1979) stated that the Killian (1971) data showed Hispanic bilingual children to be deficient in comprehending sentences and related picture materials, and quoted Killian as stating that this deficiency might have arisen from the economic impoverishment of bilingual-background children and the differences between their and other children's sociocultural experiences. These critical variables may have influenced the relatively lower WISC scores of the bilingual children. This question has been investigated more closely by Mercer (1977), who found that Mexican American children's WISC scores were systematically related to factors such as families' urban acculturation, socioeconomic status, family structure, and family size. Mercer (1977) has developed an assessment system, known as SOMPA, to more accurately assess Mexican American children's intelligence.

In weighing the validity of results of studies such as those reviewed here, one must consider that studies have not systematically sampled among different Hispanic subgroups, nor has the subjects' proficiency level in two languages in the studies been controlled or accounted for with precision within studies. For example, it would be expected that Chicano third-generation bilingual-background people, dominant in English rather than in Spanish, would be most likely to perform better on cognitive tests in English.

A recent psychometric study of bilinguals' cognitive abilities by Duncan and De Avila (1979) included investigation of Spanish-English bilingual children. The results of this study revealed that first-grade and third-grade children who were simultaneously high in both Spanish and English proficiency also manifested a high ability to perceptually dissemble parts of geometrical figures and to articulate different features in their drawings of human figures. Monolingual children from comparable backgrounds and grade levels who were of the same proficiency in their single language did not manifest similar high levels of cognitive ability on the tasks described. The Duncan and De Avila results are consistent with findings of other recent international studies surveyed by Cummins (1978) that have found positive enhancement of some cognitive skills among bilinguals possessing high levels of proficiency in two languages. The Cummins research strongly suggests the possibility that some kinds of enhanced cognitive skills — such as ability to disconnect words from their usual meanings — are aided by strong proficiency in two languages. The research in question suggests that the enhanced cognitive skills are not necessarily the same skills that lead to learning two languages well in the first place.

In his own recent research, Durán (1978, 1981, and 1982) has attempted to address shortcomings in bilingual research of the general sort mentioned. This work is investigating Mexican American bilinguals' and Puerto Rican bilinguals' performance on high level reasoning tasks of the sort that might occur on tests of logical thinking. To date, this work has established that bilingual college students perform better, as expected, in the language they read best, as assessed by scores on reading comprehension tests in both languages. The best reading language may or may not be the first language (generally Spanish). While this finding is what would be expected, Durán (1979) has also found preliminary evidence that some of the skills bilinguals use in abstract problem solving are probably the same regardless of the input language of the problems. Such a possibility is consistent with current cognitive research that indicates that many forms of mental knowledge applied in verbal problem solving are semi-independent or totally independent of the natural language systems used to represent problem information in verbal problems. The validity of such a conjecture would, in part, explain why bilinguals can transfer high level knowledge in problem solving across two language systems.

Notes

1. Throughout this report, reference is made to demographic and population survey data based on classification of respondents into ethnicity categories, such as "Hispanic," "White non-Hispanic," etc. There are many conceptual and methodological problems in arriving at unambiguous and meaningful ethnic classification of survey respondents. For a thorough discussion of these issues in the context of one Hispanic population—Mexican Americans—see Hernandez, Estrada, and Alvirez (1973); the general conceptual issues and problems they cite are relevant to all the survey data cited in this report.

2. The sources of educational statistics cited in *CEH, 1980* include: 1) The National Longitudinal Study of the High School Class of 1972; 2) Adult Basic and Secondary Education Program Statistics; 3) Characteristics of Students in Noncollegiate Postsecondary Schools; 4) Higher Education General Information Survey; 5) National Assessment of Educational Progress; 6) Current Population Survey; 7) Survey of Income and Education; 8) Survey of Earned Doctorates; 9) Elementary-Secondary Staff Information Report; 10) Higher Education Staff Information Report; 11) Elementary and Secondary School Survey; 12) NCES-Opening Fall Enrollment and Earned Degrees Survey. For details on the agencies sponsoring the sources cited and the nature of the sources, see *CEH, 1980*, pp. 257–268.

3. The Investigation of Form and Function in Chicano English: New Insights. September 10–12, 1981, The University of Texas at El Paso.

4. NAEP achievement test results are based on average percent of test items in an achievement area answered correctly by students. Achievement tests are not constructed to yield a total score on a test, because different students take different items in an area. Results for Hispanics vs. whites reported in the NAEP work are probably most representative of Mexican American rather than other Hispanics, since U.S. Western-region students' data were most often used in contrasts between Hispanics and whites.

5. The appropriateness of HS&B 1980 subtests as valid measures of achievement in each area cited is a question that needs further investigation. Heyns and Hilton (1982) discuss the history of design of cognitive HS&B tests and also issues surrounding their content validity of subtest measures of academic achievement.

6. A recent volume, *The Counselor as Gatekeeper* by Erikson and Shultz (1982), examines how communicative skills of college students and counselors affect the outcome of counseling interviews. This work

⌐ identifies many productive directions for research on Hispanic and other minority college students' communication skills.

7. Laosa (1977) distinguishes cognitive style from learning style. In his view, shared with a number of other researchers in the area, cognitive style is a construct referring to individuals' tendencies for interaction and cognition. In contrast, learning style reflects strategies individuals follow in actual learning situations. Learning styles need not always reflect cognitive styles.

8. Six studies involving Hispanics from the American College Testing Program (1973) are not reviewed here because they were insufficiently described. In these studies, the correlation of total ACT test scores with college grades and the correlation of high school grades with college grades were slightly higher overall than the patterns reported in this section. Total ACT test scores and high school grades combined correlated with college grades at the same overall level as reported for studies reviewed here that used combined verbal and mathematics test scores and high school grades.

9. The standard error or estimate statistic is a more appropriate statistic than the R (or R^2) statistic for assessing fit between predicted and actual criterion scores in regression analysis. While not inappropriate, use of R or R^2 to assess fit does not help in evaluating how much smaller the variance of residual scores is in comparison to the variance of the originally observed criterion scores. The interpretation given in the text of differences between the accuracy of prediction of Anglos' and Hispanics' college grades from college entrance examination scores and high school grades is conceptually sound. However, a more sensitive analysis of differences in prediction should rely on interpretation of standard error of estimate statistics. For the most part, standard error of estimate statistics was not directly available in the predictive validity studies reviewed in this report; in contrast, R^2 or R statistics were readily available for studies.

10. Reports on data summarized here were kindly provided by Dr. Jorge Dieppa, Director of the College Board Puerto Rico Office.

11. In the case of purely expository pieces on factors affecting Hispanic students' success in college, it is essential to recognize that such pieces are written typically by persons with direct experience with the phenomena they are addressing. While not research studies, such pieces embody practical concern of students, admissions staff, and administrators for difficulties Hispanics face in attaining and succeeding in college. Therefore, such expositions should not be dismissed as being less valuable than formal research studies, the latter which in any event hardly exist.

References

Aguirre, Jr., A., 1980. *Intelligence Testing Education and Chicanos.* ERIC/TM Report 76. Princeton: ERIC Clearinghouse on Tests, Measurement, and Evaluation, Educational Testing Service.

Alderman, D., 1982. Language proficiency as a moderator variable in testing academic aptitude. *Journal of Educational Psychology* 74(4), 580–587.

Alicea, V. G., and Mathis, J., 1975. *Determinants of Educational Attainment among Puerto Rican Youth in the U.S.* Washington, DC: Universidad Boricua.

Alvidres, M., and Whitworth, R., 1981. The development and validation of an entrance examination in a Mexican university. *Educational and Psychological Measurement* 41(2), 503–509.

American College Testing Program, 1973. *Assessing Students on the Way to College.* Technical Report for the ACT Assessment Program, 1. Iowa City, IA.

American College Testing Program, 1980. *College Student Profiles: Norms for the ACT Assessment, 1980–81 Edition.* Iowa City, IA.

Anastasi, A., and de Jesus, C., 1953. Language development and nonverbal IQ of Puerto Rican preschool children in New York City. *Journal of Abnormal Psychology* 48(3), 357–366.

Angoff, W., and Modu, C., 1973. *Equating the Scales of the Prueba De Aptitud Academica and the Scholastic Aptitude Test.* Research Report 3. New York: College Entrance Examination Board.

ASPIRA of America, 1976. *Social Factors in Educational Attainment among Puerto Ricans in U.S. Metropolitan Areas, 1970.* New York.

Astin, A., 1982. *Minorities in Higher Education.* San Francisco: Jossey-Bass.

Astin, H. S., and Burciaga, C. P., 1981. *Chicanos in Higher Education: Progress and Attainment.* Los Angeles: Higher Education Research Institute.

Attinasi, J., 1979. Language attitudes in a New York Puerto Rican community. In R. V. Padilla (ed.), *Bilingual Education and Public Policy in the United States.* Ypsilanti, MI: Eastern Michigan University.

Baral, D. P., 1979. Academic achievement of recent immigrants from Mexico. *NABE Journal* 3.

Boldt, R., 1969. *Concurrent Validity of the PAA and SAT for Bilingual Dade County High School Volunteers.* College Entrance Examination Board RDR–68–9, No. 3. Princeton: Educational Testing Service.

Breland, H., 1979. *Population Validity and College Entrance Measures.* Research Monograph No. 8. New York: College Entrance Examination Board.

Breland, H., and Griswold, P., 1981. *Group Comparisons for Basic Skills Measures.* College Board Report No. 81–6. New York: College Entrance Examination Board.

Brischetto, R. R., and Arciniega, T. A., 1973. Examining the examiners: A look at educators' perspectives on the Chicano student. In R. O. de la Garza, Z. A. Kruszewski, and T. A. Arciniega (eds.), *Chicanos and Native Americans.* Englewood Cliffs, NJ: Prentice-Hall.

Cabrera, Y. A., 1978. *Minorities in Higher Education: Chicanos and Others.* Niwot, CO: Sierra Publications.

Calkins, D. S., and Whitworth, R., 1974. Differential prediction of freshman grade-point average for sex and two ethnic classifications at a southwestern university. University of Texas at El Paso (Available as ERIC ED 102–199).

Cardoza, D., 1982. Culture fairness and prediction models: Is there an answer? Paper presented at the Second Symposium on Chicano Psychology. University of California at Riverside.

Carrasco, R.; Vera, A.; and Cazden, C., 1981a. Aspects of bilingual students' communicative competence in the classroom. In R. P. Durán (ed.), *Latino Language and Communicative Behavior*. Norwood, NJ: Ablex Publishing Corporation.

Carrasco, R., 1981b. Expanded awareness of student performance: A case study in applied ethnographic monitoring in a bilingual classroom. In H. Trueba. et al. (ed.), *Culture and the Bilingual Classroom*. Rowley, MA: Newbury House Publishers, Inc.

Carter, T., and Segura, R., 1971. *Mexican Americans in School: A Decade of Change*. New York: College Entrance Examination Board.

Castañeda, A.; Ramirez, M.; and Herold, J., 1972. *Culturally Democratic Learning Environments: A Cognitive Styles Approach*. Riverside, CA: Systems and Evaluation in Education.

Christiansen, R., and Livermore, G., 1979. A comparison of Anglo American and Spanish children on the WISC. *Journal of Social Psychology* 81(1), 14–15.

College Entrance Examination Board, 1980a. *ATP Guide for High Schools and Colleges, 1979–81*. New York.

College Entrance Examination Board, 1980b. *The College Board Publications, 1980–81*. New York.

College Entrance Examination Board, 1982. *Options for Excellence:* Annual Report, 1981–82. San Antonio, TX: The College Board.

Commission on the Higher Education of Minorities, 1982. *Final Report of the Commission on the Higher Education of Minorities*. Los Angeles: Higher Education Research Institute.

Cook, J., and Arthur, G., 1951. Intelligence rating of 97 Mexican American children in St. Paul, MN. *Journal of Exceptional Children* 18(1), 14–15.

Crain, R. L., and Mahard, R. E., 1978. Desegregation and black achievement: A review of the research. *Law and Contemporary Problems* 42(3).

Cummins, J., 1978. Bilingualism and the development of metalinguistic awareness. *Journal of Cross-Cultural Psychology* 9, 131–149.

Cummins, J., 1980. The entry and exit fallacy in bilingual education. *NABE Journal* 4(3).

Darcy, N., 1952. The performance of bilingual Puerto Rican children on verbal and nonverbal language tests of intelligence. *Journal of Educational Research* 45(7), 499–506.

DeBlassie, R. R., 1980. *Testing Mexican American Youth: A Nondiscriminatory Approach to Assessment*. Hingham, MA: Teaching Resources Corporation.

de los Santos, Jr.; Montemayor, J.; and Solis, Jr., A., 1980. *Mexican American/Chicano Students in Institutions of Higher Education: Access, Attrition and Achievement*. Austin: Office for Advanced Research in Hispanic Education. The University of Texas at Austin.

Dittmar, N., 1977. *A Comparative Investigation of the Predictive Validity of Admissions Criteria for Anglos, Blacks, and Mexican Americans*. Unpublished doctoral dissertation, The University of Texas at Austin.

Dornic, S., 1977. *Information Processing and Bilingualism*. No. 510, Reports from the Department of Psychology. Stockholm, Sweden: Department of Psychology, University of Stockholm.

Duncan, S. E., and De Avila, E., 1979. Bilingualism and cognition: Some recent findings. *NABE Journal* 4(1), 15–50.

Durán, R. P., 1978. *Logical Reasoning Skills of Puerto Rican Bilinguals*. Final Report to the National Institute of Education. Princeton: Educational Testing Service.

Durán, R. P., 1981. Reading comprehension and verbal deductive reasoning of bilinguals. In R. P. Durán (ed.), *Latino Language and Communicative Behavior*. Norwood, NJ: Ablex Publishing Corporation, 311–335.

Durán, R. P., 1982. An information processing approach to the study of Hispanic bilinguals' cognition. Paper presented at the Second Symposium on Chicano Psychology. University of California at Riverside.

Erickson, F., and Shultz, J., 1982. *The Counselor as Gatekeeper: Social Interaction in Interviews*. New York: Academic Press.

Evans, F., 1980. *A Study of the Relationships among Speed and Power, Aptitude Test Scores, and Ethnic Identity.* College Board Research and Development Report RDR 80–81, No. 2. Princeton: Educational Testing Service.

Ferrin, R.; Jonsen, R.; and Trimble, C., 1972. *Access to College for Mexican Americans in the Southwest.* Higher Education Report No. 6. New York: College Entrance Examination Board.

Fishman, J. A.; Cooper, R. L.; and Ma, R., 1971. *Bilingualism in the Barrio.* Bloomington: Indiana University Press.

Garth, T.; Elson, T.; and Morton, M., 1936. The administration of nonlanguage intelligence tests to Mexicans. *Journal of Abnormal and Social Psychology* 31(1), 53–58.

Gerard, H. B., and Miller, N., 1975. *School Desegregation.* New York: Plenum.

Goldman, R. E., and Hewitt, B., 1975. An investigation of test bias for Mexican American college students. *Journal of Educational Measurement,* 187–196.

Goldman, R., and Hewitt, B., 1976. Predicting the success of black, Chicano, oriental, and white college students. *Journal of Educational Measurement* 13(2), 109–117.

Goldman, R., and Widawski, M., 1976. An analysis of types of errors in the selection of minority college students. *Journal of Educational Measurement* 13(3).

Goldman, R., and Richards, R., 1974. The SAT prediction of grades for Mexican American versus Anglo American students of the University of California, Riverside. *Journal of Educational Measurement* 11(2), 129–135.

Hernández-Chávez, E., 1978. Language maintenance, bilingual education, and philosophies of bilingualism in the United States. In J. Alatis (ed.), *International Dimensions of Bilingual Education.* (GURT). Washington, DC: Georgetown University Press.

Hernandez, J.; Estrada, L.; and Alvirez, 1973. Census data and the problem of conceptually defining the Mexican American population. *Social Science Quarterly* 53, 671–687.

Herrick, E. M., 1981. Spanish-English orthographic issues in English composition. Paper presented at the conference of The Investigation of Form and Function in Mexican American (Chicano) English: New Insights. The University of Texas at El Paso.

Heyns, B., and Hilton, T. L., 1982. The cognitive tests for high school and beyond: An assessment. *Sociology of Education* 55(2/3), 89–102.

Kagan, S., and Buriel, R., 1977. Field dependence-independence and Mexican American culture and education. In J. Martinez, Jr. (ed.), *Chicano Psychology.* New York: Academic Press, 279–328.

Keston, M., and Jimenez, C., 1954. A study of the performance on English and Spanish editions of the Stanford-Binet intelligence test by Spanish American children. *Journal of Genetic Psychology* 85(2), 263–269.

Killian, L., 1971. WISC, Illinois Test of psycholinguistic abilities, and bender visual-motor gestalt test performance of Spanish American kindergarten and first-grade children. *Journal of Consulting and Clinical Psychology.*

Language Policy Task Force, 1980. Social dimensions of language use in East Harlem. Center for Puerto Rican Studies, Working Paper No. 7. New York: The City University of New York.

Laosa, L., 1975. Bilingualism in three United States' Hispanic groups: Contextual use of language by children and adults in their families. *Journal of Educational Psychology* 67(5), 617–627.

Laosa, L., 1977. Cognitive styles and learning strategies research. *Journal of Teacher Education* 3, 26–30.

Laosa, L. M., 1977b. Inequality in the classroom: Observational research on teacher-student interactions. *Aztlan International Journal of Chicano Studies Research* 8(2/3).

Laosa, L. M., 1977c. Nonbiased assessment of children's abilities: Historical antecedents and current issues. In T. Oakland (ed.), *Psychological and Educational Assessment of Minority Children.* New York: Brunner/Mazel.

Laosa, L. M., 1983. School, occupation, culture, and family: The impact of parental schooling on the parent-child relationship. *Journal of Educational Psychology* 74(6), 791–827.

La Red/The Net, Newsletter of the National Chicano Research Network, **May 1981.** Chicano Survey Report No. 5: Group naming and cultural inclinations. Institute for Social Research, University of Michigan at Ann Arbor, 3–4.

La Red/The Net, Newsletter of the National Chicano Council on Higher Education, **Fall 1982.** A special review symposium of *Minorities in Higher Education.* Supplemental Issue No. 60. Institute for Social Research, University of Michigan at Ann Arbor.

Lowman, R., and Spuck, D., 1975. Predictors of college success for the disadvantaged Mexican American. *Journal of College Student Personnel* 16, 40–48.

Lopez, R.; Madrid-Barela, A.; and Macias, R., 1976. *Chicanos in Higher Education: Status and Issues.* Monograph No. 7. Chicano Studies Center, Publications, UCLA.

Macias, R., 1979. *Mexicano/Chicano Sociolinguistic Behavior and Language Policy in the United States.* Unpublished doctoral dissertation. Georgetown University, Washington, DC.

Mahakian, C., 1939. Measuring the intelligence and reading capacity of Spanish-speaking children. *Elementary School Journal* 39(10), 760–768.

Mahard, R. E., 1978. The influence of high school racial composition on the academic achievement and college attendance of Hispanics. Unpublished paper. Santa Monica: The Rand Corporation.

Melendez, G.; Spuck, D.; Lowman, R.; Doggett, K.; and Banks, S., 1971. A proposed model for PSDS admissions. Unpublished manuscript. Claremont, CA: The Claremont College.

Mercer, J. R., 1952. IQ: The lethal label. *Psychology Today* 6(4), 44; 46–47, 95–96.

Mestre, J. P., 1981. Predicting academic achievement among bilingual Hispanic college technical students. *Educational and Psychological Measurement* 41, 1255–1264.

Mitchell, A., 1937. The effect of bilingualism in the measurement of intelligence. *Elementary School Journal* 38(1), 29–39.

Nielsen, F., and Fernandez, R. M., 1981. *Hispanic Students in American High Schools: Background Characteristics and Achievement.* Washington, DC: National Center for Education Statistics.

Nieves, L. R., 1982. Self-management instruction: An approach to retention and achievement problems in minority higher education. Unpublished paper. Princeton: Educational Testing Service, Office of Minority Education.

Oakland, T. (ed.), 1977. *Psychological and Educational Assessment of Minority Children.* New York: Brunner/Mazel.

Ogletree, E. J., 1978. Where is bilingual education going? Historical and legal perspectives. In H. La Fontaine, B. Persky, and L. H. Golubchick (eds.), *Bilingual Education.* Wayne, NJ: Avery Publishing Group, 52–57.

Olivas, M. A., 1979. *The Dilemma of Access.* Washington, DC: Howard University Press.

Olivas, M., 1981. *Research on Hispanic Education: Students, Finance, and Governance.* Program Report No. 81–B11. Palo Alto: Stanford University, Institute for Research on Education, Finance, and Governance.

Olmedo, E., 1977. Psychological testing and the Chicano: A reassessment. In J. Martinez, Jr. (ed.), *Chicano Psychology.* New York: Academic Press.

Ornstein-Galicia, J., 1981. Varieties of Southwest Spanish. In R. P. Durán (ed.), *Latino Language and Communicative Behavior.* Norwood, NJ: Ablex, 19–38.

Padilla, A., 1979. Critical factors in the testing of Hispanic Americans: A review and some suggestions for the future. Paper presented at the Testing, Teaching, and Learning Conference. Washington, DC: National Institute of Education.

Palmer, M., and Gaffney, P. D., 1972. Effects of administration of the WISC in Spanish and English and relationship of social class to performance. *Psychology in the Schools* 9(1), 61–63.

Payán, R., 1981. *Hispanic Access to Higher Education in the Southwest: A Research Proposal Submitted to JSRDC.* Berkeley, CA: Educational Testing Service.

Payán, R.; Flores, V.; Peterson, R.; Romero, F.; and Warren, J., 1982. *Hispanics in Higher Education in the Southwest: A Three-Part Program of Research on Attitudes, Access, and Achievement.* Research Prospectus, Berkeley, CA: Educational Testing Service.

Peñalosa, F., 1981. Some issues in Chicano sociolinguistics. In R. P. Durán (ed.), *Latino Language and Communicative Behavior.* Norwood, NJ: Ablex, 3–18.

Pike, L., 1980. *Implicit Guessing Strategies of GRE-Aptitude Examinees Classified by Ethnic Group and Sex.* GRE Board Professional Report GREB No. 75–10P. Princeton, NJ.

Poplack, S., 1981. Syntactic structure and social function of code-switching. In R. P. Durán (ed.), *Latino Language and Communicative Behavior.* Norwood, NJ: Ablex, 169–184.

Portes, A.; McLeod, S.; and Parker, R., 1978. *Immigrant Aspirations in Sociology of Education* 51, 241–160.

Ramirez, A., 1981. Language attitudes and the speech of Spanish-English bilingual pupils. In R. P. Durán (ed.), *Latino Language and Communicative Behavior.* Norwood, NJ: Ablex, 217–232.

Ramirez, M., and Castañeda, A., 1974. *Cultural Democracy: Bicognitive Development and Education.* New York: Academic Press.

Reyes, R., 1981. Independent convergence in Chicano and New York City Puerto Rican bilingualism. In R. P. Durán (ed.), *Latino Language and Communicative Behavior.* Norwood, NJ: Ablex, 39–48.

Rincon, E., 1979. *Test Speededness, Test Anxiety, and Test Performance: A Comparison of Mexican American and Anglo American High School Juniors.* Unpublished dissertation. University of Texas at Austin.

Rock, D., and Werts, C., 1979. *Construct Validity of the SAT Across Populations: An Empirical Confirmatory Study.* College Entrance Examination Board, RDR 78–79, No. 5. Princeton, NJ: Educational Testing Service.

Ryan, E., and Carranza, M. A., 1975. Evaluative reactions of adolescents toward speakers of standard English and Mexican American accented English. *Journal of Personality and Social Psychology* 31(5), 855–863.

Samuda, R., 1975. *Psychological Testing of American Minorities: Issues and Consequences.* New York: Harper and Row.

Sanchez, G., 1934. The implications of a basal vocabulary to the measurement of the abilities of bilingual children. *Journal of Social Psychology* 5(3), 395–402.

Sanchez, G., 1932. Group differences in Spanish-speaking children: A critical review. *Journal of Applied Psychology* 16(5), 549-558.

Santiago, I., 1978. *A Community Struggle for Equal Educational Opportunity: Aspira vs. Board of Education.* OME Monograph No. 2. Princeton, NJ: Educational Testing Service, Office for Minority Education.

Scott, C., 1976. *Longer-Term Predictive Validity of College Admission Tests for Anglo, Black, and Mexican American Students.* New Mexico Department of Educational Administration, University of New Mexico.

Shotwell, A., 1945. Arthur performance ratings of Mexican and American high-grade mental defectives. *American Journal of Mental Deficiency* 49(4), 445–449.

Sinnott, L., 1980. *Differences in Item Performance Across Groups.* ETS RR–80–3. Princeton, NJ: Educational Testing Service.

Teschner, R.; Bills, G.; and Cradock, J., 1975. *Spanish and English of United States Hispanos. A Critical, Annotated Bibliography.* Arlington, VA: Center for Applied Linguistics.

Thorndike, R. L., 1971. Concepts of culture-fairness. *Journal of Educational Measurement* 8, 63–70.

Troike, R., 1980. *Research Evidence for the Effectiveness of Bilingual Education.* Rosslyn, VA: National Clearinghouse for Bilingual Education.

U.S. Commission on Civil Rights, 1973.   *Teachers and Students, Differences in Teacher Interaction with Mexican American and Anglo Students.* Report V: Mexican American Education Study. A report of the U.S. Commission on Civil Rights. Washington, DC.

U.S. Department of Commerce, Bureau of the Census, 1980.   Persons of Spanish Origin in the United States: March 1979, *Population Characteristics*, Series P–20, No. 354. Washington, DC.

U.S. Department of Commerce, Bureau of the Census, 1981.   Persons of Spanish origin in the United States: March 1980 (Advance Report), *Population Characteristics*, Series P–20, No. 361. Washington, DC.

U.S. Department of Education, National Center for Education Statistics, 1980.   *The Condition of Education for Hispanic Americans.* Compiled and edited by G. H. Brown; N. Rosen; and M. A. Olivas. Washington, DC.

U.S. Department of Health, Education, and Welfare, National Center for Education Statistics, 1978a.   The educational disadvantage of language-minority persons in the United States, Spring 1976, No. 78 B–4. Washington, DC.

U.S. Department of Health, Education, and Welfare, National Center for Education Statistics, 1978b.   Place of birth and language characteristics of persons of Hispanic origin in the United States, Spring 1976, No. 78 B–6. Washington, DC.

Vasquez, M. J., 1978.   *Chicano and Anglo University Women: Factors Related to their Performance, Persistence, and Attrition.* Unpublished doctoral dissertation. The University of Texas at Austin.

von Maltitz, F. W., 1975.   *Living and Learning in Two Languages: Bilingual-Bicultural Education in the United States.* New York: McGraw-Hill.

Warren, J., 1976.   *Prediction of College Achievement among Mexican American Students in California.* College Board Research and Development Report. Princeton, NJ: Educational Testing Service.

Wild, C., 1980.   *A Summary of Data Collected from Graduate Record Examinations Test Takers During 1978–79.* Graduate Record Examination Board Data Summary Report No. 4. Princeton, NJ: Educational Testing Service.

Willingham, W. W. and Breland, H. M., 1982.   *Personal Qualities and College Admissions.* New York: College Entrance Examination Board.

Wolfram, W., 1972.   Overlapping influence and linguistic assimilation in second generation Puerto Rican English. In D. M. Smith and R. W. Shuy (eds), *Sociolinguistics in Cross-Cultural Analysis.* Washington, DC: Georgetown University Press, 15–46.

Zintz, M. V., 1963.   *Education Across Cultures.* Dubuque, IA: Wm. C. Brown.

Zirkel, P., 1975.   Spanish-speaking students and standardized testing. In E. Ogletree and G. Garcia (eds.), *Education of the Spanish-Speaking Urban Child.* Springfield, IL: Charles C. Thomas.

Index